WHITE HOUSE STUDIES SERIES

PRESIDENTIAL ADVISERS AND CLAIMS OF EXECUTIVE PRIVILEGE

WHITE HOUSE STUDIES SERIES

The Great Presidential Triumvirate at Home and Abroad: Washington, Jefferson and Lincoln
William D. Pederson and Frank J. Williams (Editors)
2006. ISBN: 1-60021-318-9

The First Woman President
Joseph Caruso (Editor)
2008. ISBN: 1-60021-348-0

Presidential Advisers and Claims of Executive Privilege
William A. Galvan (Editor)
2010. ISBN: 978-1-60692-552-2

WHITE HOUSE STUDIES SERIES

PRESIDENTIAL ADVISERS AND CLAIMS OF EXECUTIVE PRIVILEGE

WILLIAM A. GALVAN
EDITOR

Nova Science Publishers, Inc.
New York

For permission to use material from this book please contact us:
Telephone 631-231-7269; Fax 631-231-8175
Web Site: http://www.novapublishers.com

LIBRARY OF CONGRESS CATALOGING-IN-PUBLICATION DATA

ISBN: 978-1-60692-552-2

Available upon request

Published by Nova Science Publishers, Inc. ✢ New York

TABLE OF CONTENTS

PREFACE

This book explores the history, law and practice of U.S. presidential claims of confidentiality, detailing such cases as the Watergate and post-Watergate cases. Through the lens of the executive branch, it features claims of this executive privilege from President Ronald Reagan to President George W. Bush. In addition, this book details the role of presidential advisers as potential resources for Congress to exercise its constitutionally rooted right of access to the information it needs to perform its Article I legislative and oversight functions. This book further examines this issue by detailing why presidential advisers do not regularly testify before congressional committees and the legal and political problems that arise when Congress tries to enforce a subpoena to a presidential adviser.

Chapter 1 - Presidential claims of a right to preserve the confidentiality of information and documents in the face of legislative demands have figured prominently, though intermittently, in executive-congressional relations since at least 1792. Few such interbranch disputes over access to information have reached the courts for substantive resolution, the vast majority achieving resolution through political negotiation and accommodation. In fact, it was not until the Watergate-related lawsuits in the 1970's seeking access to President Nixon's tapes that the existence of a presidential confidentiality privilege was judicially established as a necessary derivative of the President's status in our constitutional scheme of separated powers. Of the eight court decisions involving interbranch or private information access disputes, three have involved Congress and the Executive but only one of these resulted in a decision on the merits. The *Nixon* and post-Watergate cases established the broad contours of the presidential communications privilege. Under those precedents, the privilege, which is constitutionally rooted, could be invoked by the President when asked to produce documents or other materials or information that reflect presidential decisionmaking and deliberations that he believes should remain confidential. If the President does so, the materials become presumptively privileged. The privilege, however, is qualified, not absolute, and can be overcome by an adequate showing of need. Finally, while reviewing courts have expressed reluctance to balance executive privilege claims against a congressional demand for information, they have acknowledged they will do so if the political branches have tried in good faith but failed to reach an accommodation.

Chapter 2- Since the beginning of the federal government, Presidents have called upon executive branch officials to provide them with advice regarding matters of policy and administration. While Cabinet members were among the first to play such a role, the creation of the Executive Office of the President (EOP) in 1939 and the various agencies located within that structure resulted in a large increase in the number and variety of presidential advisers. All senior staff members of the White House Office and the leaders of the various EOP agencies and instrumentalities could be said to serve as advisers to the President.

In: Presidental Advisers and Claims...
Editors: William A. Galvan
ISBN: 978-1-60692-552-2

Chapter 1

PRESIDENTIAL CLAIMS OF EXECUTIVE PRIVILEGE: HISTORY, LAW, PRACTICE AND RECENT DEVELOPMENTS

Morton Rosenberg

SUMMARY

Presidential claims of a right to preserve the confidentiality of information and documents in the face of legislative demands have figured prominently, though intermittently, in executive-congressional relations since at least 1792. Few such interbranch disputes over access to information have reached the courts for substantive resolution, the vast majority achieving resolution through political negotiation and accommodation. In fact, it was not until the Watergate-related lawsuits in the 1970's seeking access to President Nixon's tapes that the existence of a presidential confidentiality privilege was judicially established as a necessary derivative of the President's status in our constitutional scheme of separated powers. Of the eight court decisions involving interbranch or private information access disputes, three have involved Congress and the Executive but only one of these resulted in a decision on the merits. The *Nixon* and post-Watergate cases established the broad contours of the presidential communications privilege. Under those precedents, the privilege, which is constitutionally rooted, could be invoked by the President when asked to produce documents or other materials or information that reflect presidential decisionmaking and deliberations that he believes should remain confidential. If the President does so, the materials become presumptively privileged. The privilege, however, is qualified, not absolute, and can be overcome by an adequate showing of need. Finally, while reviewing courts have expressed reluctance to balance executive privilege claims against a congressional demand for information, they have acknowledged they will do so if the political branches have tried in good faith but failed to reach an accommodation.

However, until the District of Columbia Circuit's 1997 ruling in *In re Sealed Case (Espy),* and 2004 decision in *Judicial Watch* v. *Department of Justice,* these judicial decisions had left important gaps in the law of presidential privilege. Among the more significant issues left open included whether the President has to have actually seen or been familiar with the disputed matter; whether the presidential privilege encompasses documents and information developed by, or in the possession of, officers and employees in the departments and agencies of the Executive Branch; whether the privilege encompasses all communications with respect to which the President may be interested or is it confined to presidential decisionmaking and, if so, is it limited to any particular type of presidential decisionmaking; and precisely what kind of demonstration of need must be shown to justify release of materials that qualify for the privilege. The unanimous panel in *Espy*, and the subsequent reaffirmation of the principles articulated in *Espy* by *Judicial Watch*, authoritatively addressed each of these issues in a manner that may have drastically altered the future legal playing field in resolving such disputes. A more recent dispute with Congress involving the removal and replacement of nine United States Attorneys has drawn formal claims of privilege by President George W. Bush. Those privilege claims have been challenged in a civil suit brought by the House Judiciary Committee seeking declaratory and injunctive relief with respect to refusals to appear, to testify, and to provide documents by two subpoenaed present and former officials. The litigation may serve to further amplify the law in this area.

INTRODUCTION

Presidential claims of a right to preserve the confidentiality of information and documents in the face of legislative demands have figured prominently, though intermittently, in executive-congressional relations since at least 1792, when President Washington discussed with his cabinet how to respond to a congressional inquiry into the military debacle that befell General St. Clair's expedition.[1] Few such interbranch disputes over access to information have reached the courts for substantive resolution, the vast majority achieving resolution through political negotiation and accommodation.[2] In fact, it was not until the Watergate-related lawsuits in the 1970's seeking access to President Nixon's tapes that the existence of a presidential confidentiality privilege was judicially established as a necessary derivative of the President's status in our constitutional scheme of separated powers. Of the eight court decisions involving interbranch or private information access disputes,[3] three have involved Congress and the Executive[4] but only one of these resulted in a decision on the merits.[5] One other case, involving legislation granting custody of President Nixon's presidential records to the Administrator of the General Services Administration, also determined several pertinent executive privilege issues.[6] The most recent appellate court ruling, involving a private group's right of access under the Freedom of Information Act to pardon documents in the custody of the Justice Department, centered on a presidential claim of privilege which was rejected, and further clarified the law in this area.[7]

The *Nixon* and post-Watergate cases established the broad contours of the presidential communications privilege. Under those precedents, the privilege, which is constitutionally rooted, could be invoked by the President when asked to produce documents or other materials or information that reflect presidential decisionmaking and deliberations that he believes should remain confidential. If the President does so, the materials become presumptively privileged. The privilege, however, is qualified, not absolute, and can be overcome by an adequate showing of need. Finally, while reviewing courts have expressed reluctance to balance executive privilege claims against a congressional demand for information, they have acknowledged they will do so if the political branches have tried in good faith but failed to reach an accommodation.

However, until the District of Columbia Circuit's 1997 ruling in *In re Sealed Case (Espy)*[8] and its 2004 decision in *Judicial Watch* v. *Department of Justice*[9], these judicial decisions had left important gaps in the law of presidential privilege which have increasingly become focal points, if not the source, of interbranch confrontations that has made their resolution more difficult. Among the more significant issues left open included whether the President has to have actually seen or been familiar with the disputed matter; whether the presidential privilege encompasses documents and information developed by, or in the possession of, officers and employees in the departments and agencies of the Executive Branch; whether the privilege encompasses all communications with respect to which the President may be interested or is it confined to presidential decisionmaking and, if so, is it limited to any particular type of presidential decisionmaking; and precisely what kind of demonstration of need must be shown to justify release of materials that qualify for the privilege. The unanimous panel in *Espy*, and the subsequent reaffirmation of the principles articulated in *Espy* by *Judicial Watch*, authoritatively addressed each of these issues in a manner that may have drastically altered the future legal playing field in resolving such disputes.

A more recent dispute with Congress involving the removal and replacement of nine United States Attorneys has drawn formal claims of privilege by President George W. Bush. Those privilege claims have been challenged in a civil suit brought by the House Judiciary Committee seeking declaratory and injunctive relief with respect to refusals to appear, to testify, and to provide documents by two subpoenaed present and former officials. The litigation may serve to further amplify the law in this area. It is useful, however, before proceeding with a description and explication of *Espy* and *Judicial Watch*,and the pending civil enforcement proceeding, to review and understand the prior case law and how it has affected the positions of the disputants.

The Watergate Cases

In interbranch information disputes since the early 1980's, executive statements and positions taken in justification of assertions of executive privilege have frequently rested upon explanations of executive privilege made by the courts. To better understand the executive's stance in this area, and the potential impact on those positions by the *Espy* and *Judicial Watch* rulings, we will chronologically examine the development of the judiciary's approach and describe how the executive has adapted the judicial explanations of the privilege to support its arguments.

In *Nixon* v. *Sirica*,[10] the first of the Watergate cases, a panel of the District of Columbia Circuit rejected President Nixon's claim that he was absolutely immune from all compulsory process whenever he asserted a formal claim of executive privilege, holding that while presidential conversations are "presumptively privileged,"[11] the presumption could be overcome by an appropriate showing of public need by the branch seeking access to the conversations. In *Sirica,* "a uniquely powerful," albeit undefined, showing was deemed to have been made by the Special Prosecutor that the tapes subpoenaed by the grand jury contained evidence necessary to carrying out the vital function of determining whether probable cause existed that those indicted had committed crimes.[12]

The D.C. Circuit next addressed the Senate Watergate Committee's effort to gain access to five presidential tapes in *Senate Select Committee on Presidential Campaign Activities v. Nixon.*[13] The appeals court initially determined that "[t]he staged decisional structure established in *Nixon v. Sirica*" was applicable "with at least equal force here."[14] Thus in order to overcome the presumptive privilege and require the submission of materials for court review, a strong showing of need had to be established. The appeals court held that the Committee had not met its burden of showing that "the subpoenaed evidence is demonstrably critical to the responsible fulfillment of the Committee's function."[15] The court held that, in view of the initiation of impeachment proceedings by the House Judiciary Committee, the overlap of the investigative objectives of both committees, and the fact that the impeachment committee already had the tapes sought by the Senate Committee, "the Select Committee's immediate *oversight* need for the subpoenaed tapes is, from a congressional perspective, merely cumulative."[16] Nor did the court feel that the Committee had shown that the subpoenaed materials were "critical to the performance of [its] *legislative functions.*"[17] The court could discern "no specific legislative decisions that cannot responsibly be made without access to materials uniquely contained in the tapes or without resolution of the ambiguities that the [presidentially released] transcripts may contain."[18] The court concluded that the subsequently initiated and nearly completed work of the House Judiciary Committee had in effect preempted the Senate Committee: "More importantly,.., there is no indication that the findings of the House Committee on the Judiciary and, eventually the House of Representatives itself, are so likely to be inconclusive or long in coming that the Select Committee needs immediate access of its own."[19]

The D.C. Circuit's view in *Senate Select Committee* that the Watergate committee's oversight need for the requested materials was "merely cumulative" in light of the then concurrent impeachment inquiry, has been utilized by the Executive as the basis for arguing that the Congress' interest in executive information is less compelling when a committee's function is oversight than when it is considering specific legislative proposals.[20] This approach, however, arguably misreads the carefully circumscribed holding of the court, and would seem to construe too narrowly the scope of Congress' investigatory powers.

The *Senate Select Committee* court's opinion took great pains to underline the unique and limiting nature of the case's factual and historical context. Thus it emphasized the overriding nature of the "events that have occurred since this litigation was begun and, indeed, since the District Court issued its decision."[21]

These included the commencement of impeachment proceedings by the House Judiciary Committee, a committee with an "express constitutional source," whose "investigative objectives substantially overlap" those of the Senate Committee; that the House Committee was presently in possession of the very tapes sought by the Select Committee, making the Senate Committee's need for the tapes "from a congressional perspective, merely cumulative;" the lack of evidence indicating that Congress itself attached any particular value to "having the presidential conversations scrutinized by two committees simultaneously;" that the necessity for the tapes in order to make "legislative judgments has been substantially undermined by subsequent events," including the public release of transcripts of the tapes by the President; the transfer of four of five of the original tapes to the district court; and the lack of any "indication that the findings of the House Committee on the Judiciary and, eventually, the House of Representatives itself, are so likely to be inconclusive or long in coming that the Select Committee needs immediate access of its own."[22] The appeals court concluded by reiterating the uniqueness of the case's facts and temporal circumstances: "We conclude that the need demonstrated by the Select Committee in the peculiar circumstances of this case, including the subsequent and on-going investigation of the House Judiciary Committee, is too attenuated and too tangential to its functions to permit a judicial judgment that the President is required to comply with the Committee's subpoena."[23]

The Executive's position arguably ignores the roots of Congress' broad investigatory powers that reach back to the establishment of the Constitution and which have been continually reaffirmed by the Supreme Court. As George Mason recognized at the Constitutional Convention, Congress "are not only Legislators but they possess inquisitorial power. They must meet frequently to inspect the Conduct of the public offices."[24] Woodrow Wilson remarked:

> Quite as important as legislation is vigilant oversight of administration; and even more important than legislation is the instruction and guidance in political affairs which the people might receive from a body which kept all national concerns suffused in a broad daylight of discussion .... The informing functions of Congress should be preferred even to its legislative function. The argument is not only that a discussed and interrogated administration is the only pure and efficient administration, but, more than that, that the only really self-governing people is that people which discusses and interrogates its administration.[25]

The Supreme Court has cited Wilson favorably on this point.[26] Moreover, the Court has failed to make any distinction between Congress' right to executive branch information in pursuit of its oversight function and in support of its responsibility to enact, amend, and repeal laws. In fact, the Court has recognized that Congress' investigatory power "comprehends probes into departments of the Federal Government to expose corruption, inefficiency or waste."[27] Thus, to read *Senate Select Committee* as downplaying the status of oversight arguably ignores the court's very specific reasons for not enforcing the committee's subpoena under the unique circumstance of that case and creates a distinction between oversight and legislating that has yet to be embraced by the courts. Moreover, the *Senate Select Committee* panel's "demonstrably critical" standard for overcoming a president's presumptive claim of privilege is not reflected in any of the subsequent Supreme Court or appellate court rulings establishing a balancing test for overcoming the qualified presidential privilege.

Two months after the ruling in *Senate Select Committee,* the Supreme Court issued its unanimous ruling in *United States v. Nixon,*[28] which involved a judicial trial subpoena to the President at the request of the Watergate Special Prosecutor for tape recordings and documents relating to the President's conversations with close aides and advisors. For the first time, the Court found a constitutional basis for the doctrine of executive privilege in "the supremacy of each branch within its own assigned area of constitutional duties" and in the separation of powers.[29] But although it considered a president's communications with his close advisors to be "presumptively privileged," the Court rejected the President's contention that the privilege was absolute, precluding judicial review whenever it is asserted.[30] Also, while acknowledging the need for confidentiality of high level communications in the exercise of Article II powers, the Court stated that when the privilege depends solely on the broad, undifferentiated claim of public interest in the confidentiality of such communications," a confrontation with other values arises."[31] It held that "absent a need to protect military, diplomatic, or sensitive national security secrets, we find it difficult to accept the argument that even the very important interest in confidentiality of presidential communications is significantly diminished by production of" materials that are essential to the enforcement of criminal statutes.[32]

Having concluded that the claim of privilege was qualified, the Court resolved the "competing interests" — the President's need for confidentiality vs. the judiciary's need for materials in a criminal proceeding — "in a manner that preserves the essential functions of each branch,"[33] holding that the judicial need for the tapes, as shown by a "demonstrated, specific need for evidence in a pending criminal trial," outweighed the President's "generalized interest in confidentiality ...".[34] The Court was careful, however, to limit the scope of its decision, noting that "we are not here concerned with the balance between the President's generalized interest in confidentiality ... and congressional demands for information."[35]

In the last of the *Nixon* cases, *Nixon* v. *Administrator of General Services*[36], the Supreme Court again balanced competing interests in President Nixon's White House records. The Presidential Recordings and Materials Preservation Act granted custody of President Nixon's presidential records to the Administrator of the General Services Administration who would screen them for personal and private materials, which would be returned to Mr. Nixon, but preserve the rest for historical and governmental objectives. The Court rejected Mr. Nixon's challenge to the act, which included an argument based on the "presidential privilege of confidentiality."[37] Although *Nixon* II did not involve an executive response to a congressional probe, several points emerge from the Court's discussion that bear upon Congress' interest in confidential executive branch information. First, the Court reiterated that the executive privilege it had announced in *Nixon* I was not absolute, but qualified.[38] Second, the Court stressed the narrow scope of that privilege. "In [*Nixon* I] the Court held that the privilege is limited to communications "in performance of [a President's] responsibilities ... of his office' ... and made in the process of shaping policies and making decisions."'[39] Third, the Court found that there was a "substantial public interest[]" in preserving these materials so that Congress, pursuant to its "broad investigative power," could examine them to understand the events that led to President Nixon's resignation "in order to gauge the necessity for remedial legislation."[40]

Post-Watergate Cases

Two post-Watergate cases, both involving congressional demands for access to executive information, demonstrate both the judicial reluctance to involve itself in the essentially political confrontations such disputes represent, but also the willingness to intervene where the political process appears to be failing.

In *United States v. AT&T,*[41] the D.C. Circuit was unwilling to balance executive privilege claims against a congressional demand for information unless and until the political branches had tried in good faith but failed to reach an accommodation.[42] In that case, the Justice Department had sought to enjoin AT&T's compliance with a subpoena issued by a House subcommittee. The subcommittee was seeking FBI letters requesting AT&T's assistance with warrantless wiretaps on U.S. citizens allegedly made for national security purposes. The Justice Department argued that the executive branch was entitled to sole control over the information because of "its obligation to safeguard the national security."[43] The House of Representatives, as intervenor, argued that its rights to the information flowed from its constitutionally implied power to investigate whether there had been abuses of the wiretapping power. The House also argued that the court had no jurisdiction over the dispute because of the Speech or Debate Clause.

The court rejected the "conflicting claims of the [Executive and the Congress] to absolute authority."[44] With regard to the executive's claim, the court noted that there was no absolute claim of executive privilege against Congress even in the area of national security:

> The executive would have it that the Constitution confers on the executive absolute discretion in the area of national security. This does not stand up. While the Constitution assigns to the President a number of powers relating to national security, including the function of commander in chief and the power to make treaties and appoint Ambassadors, it confers upon Congress other powers equally inseparable from the national security, such as the powers to declare war, raise and support armed forces and, in the case of the Senate, consent to treaties and the appointment of ambassadors.[45]

Likewise, the court rejected the congressional claim that the Speech or Debate Clause was "intended to immunize congressional investigatoryactions from judicial review. Congress' investigatory power is not, itself, absolute."[46]

According to the court, judicial intervention in executive privilege disputes between the political branches is improper unless there has been a good faith but unsuccessful effort at compromise.[47] There is in the Constitution, the court held, a duty that the executive and Congress attempt to accommodate the needs of each other:

> The framers, rather than attempting to define and allocate all governmental power in minute detail, relied, we believe, on the expectation that where conflicts in scope of authority arose between the coordinate branches, a spirit of dynamic compromise would promote resolution of the dispute in the manner most likely to result in efficient and effective functioning of our governmental system.

> Under this view, the coordinate branches do not exist in an exclusively adversary relationship to one another when a conflict in authority arises. Rather, each branch should take cognizance of an implicit constitutional mandate to seek optimal accommodation through a realistic evaluation of the needs of the conflicting branches in the particular fact situation.[48]

The court refused to resolve the dispute because the executive and the Congress had not yet made that constitutionally mandated effort at accommodation. Instead, the court "encouraged negotiations in order to avoid the problems inherent in [the judiciary] formulating and applying standards for measuring the relative needs of the [executive and legislative branches]."[49] The court suggested, however, that it would resolve the dispute if the political branches failed to reach an accommodation.[50] The court-encouraged negotiations ultimately led to a compromise. Subcommittee staff was allowed to review some unedited memoranda describing the warrantless wiretaps and report orally to subcommittee members. The Justice Department retained custody of the documents.[51]

The federal district court in the District of Columbia displayed the same reluctance to intervene in an executive privilege dispute with Congress in *United States v. House of Representatives.*[52] There the court dismissed a suit brought by the Justice Department seeking a declaratory judgment that the Administrator of the Environmental Protection Agency (EPA) "acted lawfully in refusing to release certain documents to a congressional subcommittee" at the direction of the President.[53] The Administrator based her refusal upon President Reagan's invocation of executive privilege against a House committee probing the EPA's enforcement of hazardous waste laws. The court dismissed the case, without reaching the executive privilege claim, on the ground that judicial intervention in a dispute "concerning the respective powers of the Legislative and Executive Branches ... should be delayed until all possibilities for settlement have been exhausted."[54] "Compromise and cooperation, rather than confrontation, should be the aim of the parties." [55] As the Court of Appeals had done in *United States v. AT&T*, the district court in *United States v. House of Representatives* encouraged the political branches to settle their dispute rather than invite judicial intervention. Only if the parties could not agree would the court intervene and resolve the interbranch dispute, and even then, the courts advised, "Judicial resolution of this constitutional claim...will never become necessary unless Administrator Gorsuch becomes a defendant in either a criminal contempt proceeding or other legal action taken by Congress."[56] Ultimately the branches did reach an agreement, and the court did not need to balance executive and congressional interests.[57]

Executive Branch Positions on the Scope of Executive Privilege: Reagan through George W. Bush

Not surprisingly, the executive branch has developed an expansive view of executive privilege in congressional investigations, taking maximum advantage of the vague and essentially undefined terrain within the judicially recognized contours of the privilege. Thus, executive branch statements have identified four areas that are asserted to be presumptively covered by executive privilege: foreign relations and military affairs, two separate topics that are sometimes lumped together as "state secrets," law enforcement investigations, and confidential information that reveals the executive's "deliberative process" with respect to policymaking. Typically, the executive has asserted executive privilege based upon a combination of the deliberative process exemption and one or more of the other categories. As a consequence, much of the controversy surrounding invocation of executive privilege has centered on the scope of the deliberative process exemption. The executive has argued that at its core this category protects confidential predecisional deliberative material.[58] Justifications for this exemption often draw upon the language in *United States v. Nixon* that identifies a constitutional value in the President receiving candid advice from his subordinates and awareness that any expectation of subsequent disclosure might temper needed candor.[59] The result has been a presumption by the executive that its predecisional deliberations are beyond the scope of congressional demand. "Congress will have a legitimate need to know the preliminary positions taken by Executive Branch officials during internal deliberations only in the rarest of circumstances." [60] According to this view, the need for the executive to prevent disclosure of its deliberations is at its apex when Congress attempts to discover information about ongoing policymaking within the executive branch. In that case, the executive has argued, the deliberative process exemption serves as an important boundary marking the separation of powers. When congressional oversight "is used as a means of participating directly in an ongoing process of decisionmaking within the Executive Branch, it oversteps the bounds of the proper legislative function."[61]

The executive has also argued that because candor is the principal value served by the exemption, its protection should extend beyond predecisional deliberations to deliberations involving decisions already made. "Moreover, even if the decision at issue had already been made, disclosure to Congress could still deter the candor of future Executive Branch deliberations."[62] Executives have also taken the position that the privilege covers confidential communications with respect to policymaking well beyond the confines of the White House and the President's closest advisors. The Eisenhower Administration took the most expansive approach, arguing that the privilege applied broadly to advice on official matters among employees of the executive branch.[63] The Nixon Administration appears to have taken a similar view, arguing that the privilege applied to decisionmaking at a "high governmental level," but conceding that the protected communication must be related to presidential decisionmaking.[64] The Reagan Justice Department appears to have taken a slightly narrower view of the scope of the privilege, requiring that the protected communications have some nexus to the presidential decisionmaking process.[65]

The George H. W. Bush Administration took the position that recommendations made to senior department officials and communications of senior policymakers throughout the executive branch were protected by executive privilege without regard to whether they involved communications intended to go to the President.[66] Finally, the Clinton Administration took a similarly expansive position that all communications within the White House[67] or between the White House and any federal department or agency[68] are presumptively privileged.

The George W. Bush Administration, through presidential signing statements, [69] executive orders[70], and opinions of the Department of Justice's Office of Legal Counsel (OLC) has articulated a legal view of the breadth and reach of presidential constitutional prerogatives that if applied to information and documents often sought by congressional committees, would stymie such inquiries.[71] In OLC's view, under the precepts of executive privilege and the unitary executive, Congress may not bypass the procedures the President establishes to authorize disclosure to Congress of classified, privileged, or even non-privileged information by vesting lower-level officers or employees with a right to disclose such information without presidential authorization. Thus, OLC has declared that "right of disclosure" statutes "unconstitutionally limit the ability of the President and his appointees to supervise and control the work of subordinate officers and employees of the Executive Branch."[72] The OLC assertions of these broad notions of presidential prerogatives are unaccompanied by any authoritative judicial citations.

The executive has acknowledged some limits to its use of executive privilege. Thus, presidents have stated they will not use executive privilege to block congressional inquiries into allegations of fraud, corruption, or other illegal or unethical conduct in the executive branch. The Clinton Administration announced that "[i]n circumstances involving communications relating to investigations of personal wrongdoing by government officials, it is our practice not to assert executive privilege, either in judicial proceedings or in congressional investigations and hearings."[73] Similarly, the Reagan Administration policy was to refuse to invoke executive privilege when faced with allegations of illegal or unethical conduct: "[T]he privilege should not be invoked to conceal evidence of wrongdoing or criminality on the part of executive officers."[74] A significant application of this policy came in the Iran/Contra investigations when President Reagan did not assert executive privilege and even made "relevant excerpts" of his personal diaries available to congressional investigators.[75]

The executive has often tied its willingness to forego assertion of privilege claims to the recognized exceptions to the deliberative process exemption, stating that it would not seek to protect materials whose disclosure "would not implicate or hinder" the executive decisionmaking processes.[76] Thus, "factual, nonsensitive materials — communications from the Attorney General [or other executive branch official] which do not contain advice, recommendations, tentative legal judgments, drafts of documents, or other material reflecting deliberative or policymaking processes — do not fall within the scope of materials for which executive privilege may be claimed as a basis of nondisclosure."[77]

Recent administrations have stated that their policy "is to comply with congressional requests for information to the fullest extent consistent with the constitutional and statutory obligations of the Executive Branch."[78] Executive privilege will be invoked only after "careful review"[79] in the "most compelling circumstances,"[80] and only after the executive has done "the utmost to reach an accommodation" with Congress.[81] The George W. Bush Administration limited the formal claims of executive privilege to those instances where the effort to accommodate had failed and Congress had issued a subpoena.[82] The duty to seek an accommodation is said to have been the result of the uncertain boundaries between executive and legislative interests.[83] This uncertainty imposes upon each of the branches an "obligation ... to accommodate the legitimate needs of the other,"[84] and a duty to conduct "good faith" negotiations.[85] Avoiding the disclosure of embarrassing information is not a sufficient reason to withhold information from Congress.[86] In fact it has been averred that invocation of the privilege should not even be considered in the absence of a "demonstrable justification that Executive withholding will further the public interest."[87]

Where negotiations have faltered and the President has made a formal claim of executive privilege, the executive will likely argue (as the Clinton Administration did in its invocations of executive privilege[88]) that the investigating committee has not made the showing required under *Senate Select Committee v. Nixon* that the subpoenaed evidence is "demonstrably critical to the responsible fulfillment of the Committee's functions."[89] As has been indicated above, since at least the Reagan Administration, each executive has argued that Congress's interest in executive information is less compelling when the Committee's function is oversight than when it is considering specific legislative proposals.

In sum, then, in the absence of further judicial definition of executive privilege since the Nixon cases, the executive, through presidential signing statements, executive orders, Office of Legal Counsel Opinions, and, most recently, White House Counsel directives, has attempted to effect a practical expansion of the scope of the privilege. The key vehicle has been the notion of deliberative process. Developed under the Freedom of Information Act to provide limited protection for the predecisional considerations of agency officials, it has been melded with the recognized presidential interest in confidentiality of his communications with his close advisors to include pre- and post-decisional deliberations and the factual underpinnings of those decisional processes, and is argued to reach policy deliberations and communications of department and agency officials and employees in which the President may have an interest. The Clinton Administration sought to make this doctrinal expansion effective by centralizing scrutiny and control of all potential claims of executive privilege in the White House Counsel's Office. In a memorandum dated September 28, 1994, from White House Counsel Lloyd Cutler to all department and agency general counsels, agency heads were instructed to directly notify the White House Counsel of any congressional request for "any document created in the White House ... or in a department or agency, that contains deliberations of, or advice to or from the White House" which may raise privilege issues. The White House Counsel is to seek an accommodation and if that does not succeed, he is to consult with the Attorney General to determine whether to recommend invocation of privilege to the President. The President then determines whether to claim privilege, which is then communicated to the Congress by the White House Counsel.[90]

The Cutler memo modifies President Reagan's 1982 establishment of a more decentralized procedure. Under the Reagan memorandum if the head of an agency, with the advice of agency counsel, decided that a substantial question was raised by a congressional information request, the Attorney General, through the Office of Legal Counsel, and the White House Counsel's Office, was promptly notified and consulted. If one or more of the presidential advisors deemed the issue substantial, the President was informed and decided, and the decision was to be communicated by the agency head to the Congress. The Reagan memo also contrasts with the Cutler memo in that it had a far narrower definition of what the privilege covered. The Reagan memo pinpointed national security, deliberative communications that form part of the decisionmaking process, and other information important to the discharge of Executive Branch constitutional responsibilities.[91]

Establishing the White House Counsel's Office as a central clearinghouse and control center for presidential privilege claims appears to have had the effect of diminishing the historic role of the Justice Department's Office of Legal Counsel as the constitutional counselor to the President and limiting agencies' ability to deal informally with their congressional overseers, which is likely to have been its principal objective. An apparent consequence during the Clinton years was a more rapid escalation of individual interbranch information disputes clashes, a widening and hardening of the differences in the legal positions of the branches on privilege issues, and an increased difficulty in resolving disputes informally and quickly. President Clinton formally asserted executive privilege fourteen times and resolved a number of disputes under the pressure of imminent committee actions on contempt citations and subpoena issuances.[92] In addition, the Clinton Administration litigated, and lost, significant privilege cases between 1997 and 1998.[93] One, *Espy,* to which we now turn, arguably undermines many key executive assumptions about the privilege just detailed and thus may reshape the nature and course of future presidential privilege disputes.

Implications and Potential Impact of the *Espy* and *Judicial Watch* Rulings for Future Executive Privilege Disputes

In *Espy,*[94] the appeals court addressed several important issues left unresolved by the Watergate cases: the precise parameters of the presidential executive privilege; how far down the chain of command the privilege reaches; whether the President has to have seen or had knowledge of the existence of the documents for which he claims privilege; and what showing is necessary to overcome a valid claim of privilege.

The case arose out of an Office of Independent Counsel (OIC) investigation of former Agriculture Secretary Mike Espy. When allegations of improprieties by Espy surfaced in March of 1994, President Clinton ordered the White House Counsel's Office to investigate and report to him so he could determine what action, if any, he should undertake. The White House Counsel's Office prepared a report for the President, which was publically released on October 11, 1994. The *Espy* court noted that the President never saw any of the underlying or supporting documents to the report. Espy had announced his resignation on October 3, to be effective on December 31. The Independent Counsel was appointed on September 9 and the grand jury issued a subpoena for all documents that were accumulated or used in preparation of the report on October 14, three days after the report's issuance. The President withheld 84 documents, claiming both the executive and deliberative process privileges for all documents. A motion to compel was resisted on the basis of the claimed privileges. After *in camera* review, the district court quashed the subpoena, but in its written opinion the court did not discuss the documents in any detail and provided no analysis of the grand jury's need for the documents. The appeals court panel unanimously reversed.

At the outset, the court's opinion carefully distinguishes between the "presidential communications privilege" and the "deliberative process privilege." Both, the court observed, are executive privileges designed to protect the confidentiality of executive branch decisionmaking. But the deliberative process privilege, that applies to executive branch officials generally, is a common law privilege which requires a lower threshold of need to be overcome, and "disappears altogether when there is any reason to believe government misconduct has occurred."[95]

On the other hand, the court explained, the presidential communications privilege is rooted in "constitutional separation of powers principles and the President's unique constitutional role" and applies only to "direct decisionmaking by the President."[96] The privilege may be overcome only by a substantial showing that "the subpoenaed materials likely contain[] important evidence" and that "the evidence is not available with due diligence elsewhere."[97] The presidential privilege applies to all documents in their entirety[98] and covers final and post-decisional materials as well as pre-deliberative ones.[99]

Turning to the chain of command issue, the court held that the presidential communications privilege must cover communications made or received by presidential advisers in the course of preparing advice for the President even if those communications are not made directly to the President. The court rested its conclusion on "the President's dependence on presidential advisers and the inability of the deliberative process privilege to provide advisers with adequate freedom from the public spotlight" and "the need to provide sufficient elbow room for advisers to obtain information from all knowledgeable sources."[100] Thus the privilege will "apply both to communications which these advisers solicited and received from others as well as those they authored themselves. The privilege must also extend to communications authored or received in response to a solicitation by members of a presidential adviser's staff."[101]

The court, however, was acutely aware of the dangers to open government that a limitless extension of the privilege risks and carefully cabined its reach by explicitly confining it to White House staff, and not staff in the agencies, and then only to White House staff that has "operational proximity" to direct presidential decisionmaking.

> We are aware that such an extension, unless carefully circumscribed to accomplish the purposes of the privilege, could pose a significant risk of expanding to a large swath of the executive branch a privilege that is bottomed on a recognition of the unique role of the President. In order to limit this risk, the presidential communications privilege should be construed as narrowly as is consistent with ensuring that the confidentiality of the President's decisionmaking process is adequately protected. Not every person who plays a role in the development of presidential advice, no matter how remote and removed from the President, can qualify for the privilege. In particular, the privilege should not extend to staff outside the White House in executive branch agencies. Instead, the privilege should apply only to communications authored or solicited and received by those members of an immediate White House advisor's staff who have broad and significant responsibility for investigation and formulating the advice to be given the President on the particular matter to which the communications relate. Only communications at

> that level are close enough to the President to be revelatory of his deliberations or to pose a risk to the candor of his advisers. *See* AAPS, 997 F.2d at 910 (it is "operational proximity" to the President that matters in determining whether "[t]he President's confidentiality interests" is implicated)(emphasis omitted).
> Of course, the privilege only applies to communications that these advisers and their staff author or solicit and receive in the course of performing their function of advising the President on official government matters. This restriction is particularly important in regard to those officials who exercise substantial independent authority or perform other functions in addition to advising the President, and thus are subject to FOIA and other open government statutes. See *Armstrong v. Executive Office of the President,* 90 F.3d 553, 558 (D.C. Cir. 1996), *cert denied* — U.S. — -, 117 S.Ct. 1842, 137 L. Ed.2d 1046 (1997). The presidential communications privilege should never serve as a means of shielding information regarding governmental operations that do not call ultimately for direct decisionmaking by the President. If the government seeks to assert the presidential communications privilege in regard to particular communications of these "dual hat" presidential advisers, the government bears the burden of proving that the communications occurred in conjunction with the process of advising the President.[102]

The appeals court's limitation of the presidential communications privilege to "direct decisionmaking by the President" makes it imperative to identify the type of decisionmaking to which it refers. A close reading of the opinion makes it arguable that it is meant to encompass only those functions that form the core of presidential authority, involving what the court characterized as "quintessential and non-delegable Presidential power."[103] In the case before it, the court was specifically referring to the President's Article II appointment and removal power which was the focal point of the advice he sought in the Espy matter. But it seems clear from the context of the opinion that the description was meant to be in juxtaposition with the appointment and removal power and in contrast with "presidential powers and responsibilities" that "can be exercised or performed without the President's direct involvement, pursuant to a presidential delegation of authority or statutory framework."[104] The reference the court uses to illustrate the latter category is the President's Article II duty "to take care that the laws are faithfully executed," a constitutional direction that the courts have consistently held not to be a source of presidential power but rather an obligation on the President to see to it that the will of Congress is carried out by the executive bureaucracy.[105]

The appeals court, then, would appear to be confining the parameters of the newly formulated presidential communications privilege by tying it to those Article II functions that are identifiable as "quintessential and non-delegable," which would appear to include, in addition to the appointment and removal powers, the commander-in-chief power, the sole authority to receive ambassadors and other public ministers, the power to negotiate treaties, and the power to grant pardons and reprieves. On the other hand, decisionmaking vested by statute in the President or agency heads such as rulemaking, environmental policy, consumer protection, workplace safety and labor relations, among others, would not necessarily be covered. Of course, the President's role in supervising and coordinating (but not displacing) decisionmaking in the executive branch remains unimpeded. But his communications in furtherance of such activities would presumably not be cloaked by constitutional privilege.

Such a reading of this critical passage of the court's opinion is consonant with the court's view of the source and purpose of the presidential communications privilege and its expressed need to confine it as narrowly as possible. Relying on *Nixon I,* the *Espy* court identifies "the President's Article II powers and responsibilities as the constitutional basis of the presidential communications privilege ... Since the Constitution assigns these responsibilities to the President alone, arguably the privilege of confidentiality that derives from it also should be the President's alone."[106] Again relying on *Nixon* I, the court pinpoints the essential purpose of the privilege: "[Tlhe privilege is rooted in the need for confidentiality to ensure that presidential decisionmaking is of the highest caliber, informed by honest advice and knowledge. Confidentiality is what ensures the expression of 'candid, objective, and even blunt or harsh opinions' and the comprehensive exploration of all policy alternatives before a presidential course of action is selected."[107] The limiting safeguard is that the privilege will apply in those instances where the Constitution provides that the President alone must make a decision. "The presidential communications privilege should never serve as a means of shielding information regarding governmental operations that do not call ultimately for direct decisionmaking by the President."[108]

The District of Columbia Circuit's 2004 decision in *Judicial Watch, Inc. v. Department of Justice*[109] appears to lend substantial support to the above-expressed understanding of *Espy. Judicial Watch* involved requests for documents concerning pardon applications and pardon grants reviewed by the

Justice Department's Office of the Pardon Attorney and the Deputy Attorney General for consideration by President Clinton.[110] Some 4,300 documents were withheld on the grounds that they were protected by the presidential communications and deliberative process privileges. The district court held that because the materials sought had been produced for the sole purpose of advising the President on a "quintessential and nondelegable Presidential power" — the exercise of the President's constitutional pardon authority — the extension of the presidential communications privilege to internal Justice Department documents which had not been "solicited and received" by the President or the Office of the President was warranted.[111] The appeals court reversed, concluding that "internal agency documents that are not solicited and received by the President or his Office are instead protected against disclosure, if at all, by the deliberative process privilege."[112]

Guided by the analysis of the *Espy* ruling, the panel majority emphasized that the "solicited and received" limitation "is necessitated by the principles underlying the presidential communications privilege, and a recognition of the dangers of expanding it too far."[113] *Espy* teaches, the court explained, that the privilege may be invoked only when presidential advisers in close proximity to the President, who have significant responsibility for advising him on non-delegable matters requiring direct presidential decisionmaking, have solicited and received such documents or communications or the President has received them himself. In rejecting the Government's argument that the privilege should be applicable to all departmental and agency communications related to the Deputy Attorney General's pardon recommendations for the President, the panel majority held that:

> Such a bright-line rule is inconsistent with the nature and principles of the presidential communications privilege, as well as the goal of serving the public interest .... Communications never received by the President or his Office are unlikely to "be revelatory of his deliberations ... nor is there any reason to fear that the Deputy Attorney General's candor or the quality of the Deputy's pardon recommendations would be sacrificed if the presidential communications privilege did not apply to internal documents .... Any pardon documents, reports or recommendations that the Deputy Attorney General submits to the Office of the President, and any direct communications the Deputy or the Pardon Attorney may have with the White House Counsel or other immediate Presidential advisers will remain protected .... It is only those documents and recommendations of Department staff that are not submitted by the

> Deputy Attorney General for the President and are not otherwise received by the Office of the President, that do not fall under the presidential communications privilege.[114]

Indeed, the *Judicial Watch* panel makes it clear that the *Espy* rationale would preclude cabinet department heads from being treated as being part of the President's immediate personal staff or as some unit of the Office of the President:

> Extension of the presidential communications privilege to the Attorney General's delegatee, the Deputy Attorney General, and his staff, on down to the Pardon Attorney and his staff, with the attendant implication for expansion to other Cabinet officers and their staffs, would, as the court pointed out in *In re Sealed Case*, pose a significant risk of expanding to a large swatch of the executive branch a privilege that is bottomed on a recognition of the unique role of the President.[115]

The *Judicial Watch* majority took great pains to explain why *Espy* and the case before it differed from the Nixon and post-Watergate cases. According to the court, "[u]ntil *In re Sealed Case*, the privilege had been tied specifically to direct communications of the President with his immediate White House advisors."[116] The *Espy* court, it explained, was for the first time confronted with the question whether communications that the President's closest advisors make in the course of preparing advise for the President and which the President never saw should also be covered by the presidential privilege. The *Espy* court's answer was to "espouse[ ] a 'limited extension' of the privilege' 'down the chain of command' beyond the President to his immediate White House advisors only," recognizing "the need to ensure that the President would receive full and frank advice with regard to his non-delegable appointment and removal powers, but was also wary of undermining countervailing considerations such as openness in government .... Hence, the [*Espy*] court determined that while 'communications authored or solicited and received' by immediate White House advisors in the Office of the President could qualify under the privilege, communications of staff outside the White House in executive branch agencies that were not solicited and received by such White House advisors could not."[117]

The situation before the *Judicial Watch* court tested the *Espy* principles. While the presidential decision involved — exercise of the President's pardon power — was certainly a non-delegable, core presidential function, the operating officials involved, the Deputy Attorney General and the Pardon Attorney, were deemed to be too remote from the President and his senior White House advisors to be protected. The court conceded that functionally those officials were performing a task directly related to the pardon decision, but concluded that an organizational test was more appropriate for confining the potentially broad sweep that would result from a functional test. Under the latter test, there would be no limit to the coverage of the presidential communications privilege. In such circumstances, the majority concluded, the lesser protections of the deliberative process privilege would have to suffice.[118] That privilege was found insufficient and the appeals court ordered the disclosure of the 4,300 withheld documents.

It may be noted that, in at least one analogous instance the White House divulged documents sought by a congressional committee which argued the more limited reading of *Espy.* When *Espy* was decided, the House Resources Committee was in the midst of an inquiry of President Clinton's utilization of the Antiquities Act of 1906,[119] which authorizes the President, in his discretion, to declare by public proclamation objects of historic or scientific interest on federal lands to be national monuments, by reserving parcels that "shall be confined to the smallest area compatible with the proper care and management to the objects to be protected." The act establishes no special procedures for the decision to declare a national monument and contains no provision for judicial review. Shortly before the 1996 presidential election, President Clinton reserved 1.7 million acres in Utah by proclamation. Central to the Committee's inquiry as to the propriety and integrity of the decisionmaking process that led to the issuance of the presidential proclamation were the actions of the Council on Environmental Quality (CEQ), an office within the Executive Office of the President with about the same degree of advisory proximity as that of the White House Counsel's Office. Requests for physical production of documents from CEQ met with limited compliance: an offer to view 16 documents at the White House. The Committee believed that it required physical possession in order to determine the propriety of the process and issued a subpoena which was not complied with on the return date.

During intense negotiations, the White House claimed the documents were covered by the presidential communications privilege, even as defined by *Espy.* In a letter to the Committee, the White House Counsel's Office argued that the opinion did not confine the privilege to just core Article II powers, but included presidential decisionmaking encompassed within the Article II duty to take care that the laws be faithfully executed. It asserted that since the

President had the sole authority to designate a monument by law, that decisional process, including deliberations among and advice of White House advisers, was covered. The Committee in reply letters disagreed, arguing that *Espy* would not encompass a statutory delegation of decisional authority. On the eve of a scheduled Committee vote on a resolution of contempt, the White House produced all the documents.[120]

The narrower reading of *Espy* by the House Committee also accommodates the need of Congress for flexibility in assigning tasks for executive fulfillment. It is, of course, the predominant practice of Congress to delegate the execution of laws to the heads of departments and agencies. But there are occasions when the nature of the decisionmaking is deemed so sensitive or important or unique that direct presence of presidential authority is appropriate. Where the exercise of such authority derives solely from the statutory delegation and does not find its basis in one of the so-called "core" constitutional powers of the President, it is a reasonable expectation of the Congress that it will be able to determine whether and how the legislative intent has been carried out, just as it does with its assignments to the departments and agencies. A view that any delegation of decisionmaking authority directly to the President will thereby cloak it from congressional scrutiny is not only anomalous but arguably counterproductive of interbranch coordination, cooperation and comity, as it would discourage such delegations.[121] Of course, further judicial development of the principles enunciated in *Espy* may alter this view of its scope.

Recent Developments: George W. Bush Claims of Executive Privilege

In early 2007, the House Judiciary Committee and its Subcommittee on Commercial and Administrative Law commenced an inquiry into the propriety of the termination and replacement of a number of United States Attorneys. Six hearings and numerous interviews were held by the committees between March and June 2007, essentially focusing on testimony with respect to actions of present and former Department of Justice (DOJ) officials and employees as well as DOJ documents relating to the matter. On March 21, 2007, the House Subcommittee authorized Chairman John Conyers, Jr. to issue subpoenas to a number of present and former White House Officials for documents and testimony. On June 13, 2007, Chairman Conyers issued subpoenas to White House Chief of Staff Joshua Bolten, as custodian of White

House documents, returnable on June 28, 2007, and to former White House Counsel Harriet Miers, returnable on July 12, 2007.

On June 27, 2007, White House Counsel Fred F. Fielding, at the direction of President Bush, advised the Chairmen of the House and Senate Judiciary Committees that document subpoenas issued to the White House custodian of documents and to two former White House officials, Sara M. Taylor, subpoenaed by the Senate Judiciary Comittee, and Harriet Miers, relating to those Committees investigations of the dismissal and replacement of nine U.S. attorneys in 2006, had been deemed by the President subject to executive privilege and that the subpoena recipients have been directed not to produce any documents. The Fielding letter also noted that the testimony sought from Ms. Miers and Ms. Taylor is also subject to a "valid claim of Executive Privilege," and will be asserted if the matter cannot be resolved before dates scheduled for their appearances.[122]

Accompanying the Fielding letter was a legal memorandum prepared by Acting Attorney Paul D. Clement for the President detailing the legal basis for a claim of executive privilege.[123] The memo identifies three categories of documents being sought: (1) internal White House Communications; (2) communications by White House Officials with individuals outside the Executive Branch, including individuals in the Legislative Branch; and (3) communications between White House and Justice Department officials.[124] With respect to internal White House communications, which are said consist of discussions of "the wisdom" of removal and replacement proposals, which U.S. Attorneys should be removed, and possible responses to Congressional and media inquiries, such discussions are claimed to be the "types of internal deliberations among White House officials [that] fall squarely within the scope of executive privilege" since their non-disclosure "promote[s] sound decisionmaking by ensuring that senior Government officials and their advisors may speak frankly and candidly during the decisionmaking process," citing *U.S.* v. *Nixon*. Since, it is argued, what is involved is the exercise of the presidential power to appoint and remove officers of the United States, a "quintessential and nondelegable Presidential power" (citing *Espy*), the President's protected confidentiality interests "are particularly" strong in this instance. As a consequence, an inquiring congressional committee would have to meet the standard established by the *Senate Select Committee* decision requiring a showing that the documents and information are "demonstrably critical to the responsible fulfillment of the Committee's function."[125] Thus, it is claimed, there is doubt whether the Committees have oversight authority over deliberations essential to the exercise of this core presidential power or that "their interests justify overriding a claim of executive privilege as to the matters at issue."[126]

With respect to category 2 matters involving communications by White House officials with individuals outside the White House, the Clement memo asserts that confidentiality interests undergirding the privilege are not diminished if the President or his close advisors have to go outside the White House to obtain information to make an "informed decision," particularly about a core presidential power. Again, *Espy* and *Senate Select Committee* are referred as supporting authority.

As to the final category, respecting communications between the Justice Department and the White House concerning proposals to dismiss and replace U.S. Attorneys, it is claimed that such communications "are deliberative and clearly fall within the scope of executive privilege ... [T]he President's need to protect deliberations about the selection of U.S. Attorneys is compelling, particularly given Congress' lack of legislative authority over the nomination or replacement of U.S. Attorneys," citing *Espy* and *Senate Select Committee.*[127] The privilege is asserted to extend to White House - DOJ communications "that have been previously disclosed to the Committees by the Department." An argument that a waiver may have occurred is contrary to "relevant legal principles [that] should and do encourage, rather than punish, such accommodation[s] by recognizing that Congress' need for such documents is reduced to the extent similar materials have been provided voluntarily as part of the accommodation process." Since the Committees have these documents, seeking the relevant communications would be cumulative under *Senate Select Committee.*[128] This rationale is argued to support the lack of any need for the testimony of the former White House officials subpoenaed:

> Congressional interest in investigating the replacement of U.S. Attorneys clearly falls outside its core constitutional responsibilities and any legitimate interest Congress may have in the disclosed communications has been satisfied by the Department's extraordinary accommodation involving the extensive production of documents to the Committees, interviews, and hearing testimony concerning these communications. As the D.C. Circuit has explained, because "legislative judgements normally depend more on the predicted consequences of proposed legislative actions and their political acceptability," Congress will rarely need or be entitled to a "precise reconstruction of past events" to carry out its legislative responsibilities. *Senate Select Comm.*, 498 F. 2d at 732[129]

On June 29, 2007, Chairman Conyers and Senate Judiciary Committee Chairman Patrick Leahy jointly responded to the Fielding letter and Clement memorandum. Characterizing the White House stance as "based on blanket executive privilege claims," which makes it difficult for the Committees "to determine where privilege truly does and does not apply," the Committees demanded that they be provided with a detailed privilege log that includes for each document withheld a description of the nature, source, subject matter and date of the document; the name and address of each recipient of an original or copy of the document and the date received; the name and address of each additional person to whom any of the contents of the document was disclosed, along with the date and manner of disclosure; and the specific basis for the assertion of privilege. A deadline for receipt of the privilege log was set for July 9, 2007.

On July 9, 2007, the White House Counsel refused to comply. On that same date, counsel to Ms. Miers informed Chairman Conyers that pursuant to letters received from the White House Counsel, Miers would not testify or produce documents, and the next day, July 10, announced that Miers would not appear at all. That same day the DOJ office of Legal Counsel (OLC) issued an opinion that "Ms. Miers is [absolutely] immune from compulsion to testify before the Committee on this matter and therefore is not required to appear to testify about the subject."[130] Citing previous OLC opinions, the opinion asserts that since the President is the head of one of the independent branches of the federal government, "If a congressional committee could force the President's appearance, fundamental separation of powers principles – including the President's independence and autonomy from Congress– would be threatened." As a consequence, "[t]he same separation of powers principles that protect a President from compelled congressional testimony also apply to senior presidential advisors" because such appearances would be tantamount to the President himself appearing. The fact that Ms. Miers is a former counsel to the President does not alter the analysis since, "a presidential advisor's immunity is derivative of the President's." Neither Ms. Miers nor Mr. Bolten complied on the return dates of their subpoenas.

On July 12, 2007, the House Subcommittee met and Chairman Sánchez issued a ruling rejecting Ms. Miers' privilege claims with respect to failing to appear, produce documents and testify, which was upheld by a 7-5 vote. On July 19 the Subcommittee Chair ruled against Mr. Bolten's privilege claims with respect to his failure to produce documents, which was upheld by a 7-5 vote. On July 25, the full Judiciary Committee voted, 21-17, to issue a report to the House recommending that a resolution of contempt of Congress against

Miers and Bolten be approved. Thereafter, the White House announced that it would order the United States Attorney for the District of Columbia not to present the contempt of Congress citation for grand jury consideration.

The Judiciary Committee filed its Report formally reporting a contempt violation to the House in November 2007.[131] After further attempts at accommodation failed, the matter was brought to the floor of the House on February 14, 2008, which voted 223 to 32 to hold Ms. Miers and Mr. Bolten in contempt of Congress for their willful failure to comply with the Committee's subpoenas. At the same time the House passed three resolutions. H.Res. 979 directed the Speaker to certify the report of the Judiciary Committee, detailing the refusals of Ms. Miers to appear before, to testify before, and to produce documents to the Committee and Mr. Bolten's refusal to produce documents, as required by subpoenas, to the United States Attorney for the District of Columbia for presentation to a grand jury pursuant to 2 U.S.C. 192 and 194.[132]

H.Res. 980, in apparent anticipation that the criminal contempt citation would not be presented to the grand jury by the U.S. Attorney, authorized the Chairman of the Judiciary Committee to initiate civil judicial proceedings in federal court to seek a declaratory judgment affirming the duty of any individual to comply with any subpoena that is the subject of H.Res. 979 and to issue appropriate injunctions to achieve compliance. The resolution also authorized the House General Counsel to represent the Committee in any such litigation. H.Res. 982 adopted both H.Res. 979 and H.Res. 980.

On February 28, 2008, the Speaker certified the Committee's Report to the U.S. Attorney. On February 29, 2008, Attorney General Mukasey advised the Speaker that "the Department will not bring the congressional contempt citations before a grand jury or take any other action to prosecute Mr. Bolten or Ms. Miers."

On March 10, 2008, the House General Counsel filed a civil action for declaratory judgement and injunctive relief against Ms. Miers and Mr. Bolten.[133] The suit seeks a declaration by the court that (1) Ms. Miers is not immune from the obligation to appear before the Committee in response to a duly authorized, issued and served Committee subpoena; (2) Ms. Miers and Mr. Bolten produce privilege logs identifying all documents withheld on grounds of executive privilege; and (3) Ms. Miers and Mr. Bolten's claims are improper in the context of communications not involving the President or undertaken directly in preparation for advising the President and that Ms. Miers and Mr. Bolten's claims of executive privilege are, in any event, overcome by the Committee's demonstrated, specific need for the subpoenaed testimony and comments. In addition, the Committee seeks an order directing

Ms. Miers to appear before the Committee to respond to questions and to invoke executive privilege if and when appropriate; to have Ms. Miers and Mr. Bolten provide detailed privilege logs with respect to documents claimed to be privileged and for both to produce all non-privileged documents subject to the subpoenas.

On April 10, 2008, the House General Counsel filed a Motion for Partial Summary Judgment seeking a declaration that (1) Ms. Miers failure to appear at all in response to the Committee's subpoena was without legal justification; (2) that she must appear before the Committee and assert privilege claims in response to questions, as appropriate, but must testify about subjects not covered by privilege; (3) that the failure of both Ms. Miers and Mr. Bolten to supply privilege logs with respect to withheld documents is legally unjustified; and (4) that both be ordered to provide detailed privilege logs with respect to documents claimed to be privileged and to produce all relevant non-privileged documents.

By agreement, the Government's response to the Committee's partial summary judgment motion is due May 9, 2008; the Committee's reply is due May 29, 2008; the Government's reply in support of any dispositive cross-motions is due by June 12, 2008; and oral argument on the motions is scheduled for June 27, 2008.

This is the third claim of executive privilege invoked by the Bush Administration.[134] The first was asserted by President Bush on December 12, 2001, directing Attorney General Ashcroft to refuse to comply with document subpoenas issued by the House Government Reform Committee as part of the investigation of alleged law enforcement corruption in the FBI's Boston Field Office over a period of almost 30 years. Following two hearings in which the validity of the privilege claim was the central issue, testimony presenting overwhelming evidence that similar DOJ documents and testimony had been provided in the face of investigative demands by jurisdictional committees for over 85 years, despite claims of interference with prosecutorial deliberations, and with a credible threat of a successful contempt vote on the floor of the House, the documents were relinquished.[135]

The second claim of privilege, apparently asserted on behalf of the President by White House Counsel Alberto Gonzales, occurred during the *Judicial Watch* litigation over the release of some 4,300 pardon documents that were in the custody of the Pardon Attorney in the Justice Department and that had never been requested by White House officials or the President. The panel majority held that in light of the *Espy* ruling, the presidential communications privilege was inapplicable and ordered the documents to be released to the requesters.

CONCLUDING OBSERVATIONS

As indicated in the above discussion, recent appellate court rulings cast considerable doubt on the broad claims of privilege posited by OLC in the past and now by the Clement Memo and the July 10, 2007, OLC opinion on witness immunity. Taken together, *Espy* and *Judicial Watch* arguably have effected important qualifications and restraints on the nature, scope and reach of the presidential communications privilege. As established by those cases, and until reviewed by the Supreme Court, the following elements appear to be essential to appropriately invoke the privilege:

1. The protected communication must relate to a "quintessential and nondelegable presidential power." *Espy* and *Judicial Watch* involved the appointment and removal and the pardon powers, respectively. Other core, direct precedential decisionmaking powers include the Commander-in-Chief power, the sole authority to receive ambassadors and other public ministers, and the power to negotiate treaties. It would arguably not include decisionmaking with respect to laws that vest policymaking and administrative implementation authority in the heads of department and agencies or which allow presidential delegations of authority.
2. The communication must be authored or "solicited and received" by a close White House advisor (or the President). The judicial test is that an advisor must be in "operational proximity" with the President. This effectively means that the scope of the presidential communications privilege extends only to the administrative boundaries of the Executive Office of the President and the White House.
3. The presidential communications privilege remains a qualified privilege that may be overcome by a showing that the information sought "likely contains important evidence" and the unavailability of the information elsewhere by an appropriate investigating authority. The *Espy* court found an adequate showing of need by the Independent Counsel; while in *Judicial Watch*, the court found the privilege did not apply, and the deliberative process privilege was unavailing.

Definitively applying the teachings of *Espy* and *Judicial Watch* to current withholding claims in a context not yet fully developed may be premature. Indeed, the House Judiciary Committee's motion for partial summary judgment appears designed to focus the court's initial attention on the claim of absolute witness immunity, which would absolve a subpoenaed official, past or present, from even being required to appear personally to claim privilege. The Committee's motion argues that the Supreme Court's ruling in *United States* v. *Nixon* [136] flatly rejected the President's claim of absolute immunity with respect to presidential communications, allowing only a qualified constitutional privilege that is presumptive when asserted but which may be overcome by a proper showing of need and unavailability elsewhere by an authorized investigating body. Subsequent Supreme Court and appellate court rulings have reiterated the qualified nature of the privilege.[137] Thus, it is contended, allowing the holder of a qualified privilege to absolutely cloak from disclosure information possessed by a source that might enable the investigative body to overcome the presumption, arguably thereby renders the privilege absolute. It may be anticipated that the Government's reply will track the OLC opinion of July 10, 2007, that contended that "[t]he same separation of powers principles that protect a President from compelled congressional testimony also apply to senior presidential advisors" because such appearances would be tantamount to the President himself appearing.[138] If the court agrees with the Committee, directs Ms. Miers to testify, and orders Ms. Miers and Mr. Bolten to provide privilege logs for withheld documents, then the question of the applicability and effect of *Espy* and *Judicial Watch* on the nature, scope, and reach of the presidential communications privilege may be tested in a subsequent phase of the litigation.

Appendix: Presidential Claims of Executive Privilege from the Kennedy Administration through the George W. Bush Administration

Following is a brief summary recounting of assertions of presidential claims of executive privilege from the Kennedy Administration through the Bush II Administration.

1. Kennedy

President Kennedy established the policy that he, and he alone, would invoke the privilege. Kennedy appears to have utilized the privilege twice with respect to information requests by congressional committees. In 1962, the President directed the Secretary of Defense not to supply the names of individuals who wrote or edited speeches requested by a Senate subcommittee investigating military Cold War education and speech review policies. The chairman of the subcommittee acquiesced to the assertion. The President also directed that his military adviser, General Maxwell Taylor, refuse to testify before a congressional committee examining the Bay of Pigs affair. See Rozell, text note 1, at 40-41.

2. Johnson

President Johnson, although he announced that he would follow the Kennedy policy of personal assertion of executive privilege, apparently did not do so in practice. Rozell, *supra*, at 41-42, catalogues three instances in which executive officials refused to comply with congressional committee requests for information or testimony which involved presidential actions, but did not claim they were directed to do so by the President.

3. Nixon

President Nixon asserted executive privilege six times. He directed Attorney General Mitchell to withhold FBI reports from a congressional committee in 1970. In 1971, Secretary of State Rogers asserted privilege at the President's direction to withhold information from Congress with respect to military assistance programs. A claim of privilege was asserted at the direction of the President to prevent a White House advisor from testifying on the IT&T settlement during the Senate Judiciary Committee's consideration of the Richard Kleindienst nomination for Attorney General in 1972. Finally, President Nixon claimed executive privilege three times with respect to subpoenas for White House tapes relating to the Watergate affair: once with respect to a subpoena from the Senate Select Committee; again with respect to a grand jury subpoena for the same tapes by Special Prosecutor Archibald

Cox; and then, with respect to a jury trial subpoena for 64 additional tapes issued by Special Prosecutor Leon Jaworski. Rozell, *supra*, at 57-62.

4. Ford and Carter

President Ford directed Secretary State Kissinger to withhold documents during a congressional committee investigation relating to State Department recommendations to the National Security Council to conduct covert activities in 1975. President Carter directed Energy Secretary Duncan to claim executive privilege in the face of a committee's demand for documents relating to the development and implementation of apolicy to impose a petroleum import fee. Rozell, *supra* at 77-82; 87-91.

5. Reagan

President Reagan directed the assertion of executive privilege before congressional committees three times: by Secretary of the Interior James Watt with respect to an investigation of Canadian oil leases (1981-82); by EPA Administrator Ann Burford with respect to Superfund enforcement practices (1982-83); and by Justice William Rehnquist during his nomination proceedings for Chief Justice with respect to memos he had written when he was Assistant Attorney for the Office of Legal Counsel in the Department of Justice (1986). Rozell, *supra*, at 98-105.

6. Bush, George H. W.

President Bush asserted privilege only once, in 1991, when he ordered Defense Secretary Cheney not to comply with a congressional subpoena for a document related to a subcommittee's investigation of cost overruns in, and cancellation of, a Navy aircraft program. Rozell, *supra*, at 108-119.

7. Clinton

President Clinton apparently discontinued the policy of issuing *written* directives to subordinate officials to exercise executive privilege. Thus, in some instances, it is not totally clear when a claim of privilege by a subordinate was orally directed by the President even if it was shortly withdrawn. The following documented assertions may arguably be deemed formal invocations. Four of the assertions occurred during grand jury proceedings. We list the individual assertions and briefly identify them.

i. Kennedy Notes (1995)(executive privilege initially raised but never formally asserted)(Senate Whitewater investigation). S.Rept. 104-191, 104th Cong., 1st Sess. (1995).
ii. White House Counsel Jack Quinn/Travelgate investigations (1996)(House Government Reform). H.Rept. 104-598, 104th Cong., 2d Sess. (1996).
iii. FBI-DEA Drug Enforcement Memo (1996)(House Judiciary)
iv. Haiti/Political Assassinations Documents (1996)(House International Relations).
v. *In re Grand Jury Subpoena Duces Tecum*, 112 F. 3d 910 (8th Cir. 1997)(executive privilege claimed and then withdrawn in the district court. Appeals court rejected applicability of common interest doctrine to communications with White House counsel's office attorneys and private attorneys for the First Lady).
vi. *Espy*, 121 F. 3d 729 (D.C. Cir. 1997)(Espy case)(executive privilege asserted but held overcome with respect to documents revealing false statements).
vii. *In re Grand Jury Proceedings*, 5 F. Supp. 2d 21 (D.D.C. 1998)(executive privilege claimed but held overcome because testimony of close advisors was relevant and necessary to grand jury investigation of Lewinski matter and was unavailable elsewhere).

The September 9, 1998, Referral to the House of Representatives by Independent Counsel Kenneth Starr detailed the following previously undisclosed presidential claims of executive privilege (viii - xiii) before grand juries that occurred during the Independent Counsel's investigations of the Hubbell and Lewinski matters. H. Doc. 105-310, 105th Cong., 2d Sess. (1998).

viii. Thomas "Mack" McLarty (1997)(claimed at direction of President
ix. Nancy Hernreich (claimed at direction of President but withdrawn prior to March 20, 1998 hearing to compel).
x. Sidney Blumenthal (claim rejected by District Court, 5 F. Supp. 2d 21 (D.D.C. 1998) dropped on appeal).

xi. Cheryl Mills (claimed on August 11, 1998).

xii. Lanny Breuer (claimed on August 4, 1998 and denied by Judge Johnson on August 11). *In re Grand Jury Proceeding*. Unpublished Order (Under Seal) (August 11, 1998).

xiii. Bruce Lindsey (claimed on August 28, 1998).

H. Doc. 105-310, 105th Cong, 2d Sess. 206-209 (1998).

xiv. FALN Clemency (claimed at direction of President by Deputy Counsel to the President Cheryl Mills on September 16, 1999 in response to subpoenas by House Government Reform Committee).

8. Bush, George W.

President Bush has thus far asserted executive privilege three times, once by written directive to the Attorney General, and twice by apparent oral directives to subordinate executive officials to claim the privilege.

i. President Bush, on December 12, 2001, ordered Attorney General Ashcroft not to comply with a congressional subpoena, for documents related to a House Committee's investigation of corruption in the FBI's Boston regional office. The documents were ultimately released shortly after the conduct of the oversight hearings by the Committee. H.Rept. 108-414, 108th Cong., 1st Sess. (2004).

ii. *Judicial Watch Inc.* v. *Department of Justice*, 365 F. 3d. 1108 (D.C. Cir. 2004) (Rejecting the claimed applicability of the presidential communications privilege to pardon documents sought under FOIA from DOJ's Office of the Pardon Attorney).

iii. Removal and Replacement of U.S. Attorneys (2007). At the direction of the President, on June 28, 2007, the White House Counsel advised the House and Senate Judiciary Committees that subpoenas issued for documents and testimony relating to the firing of U.S. Attorneys to former White House counsel Harriet Miers and Chief of Staff Joshua B. Bolten in 2006 were subject to a claim of executive privilege and that these present and former White House officials subpoenaed would be ordered not to comply or to appear at a hearing. Miers and Bolten were voted in contempt by the House on February 14, 2008, and on February 28, the Speaker transmitted the contempt citation to the U.S. Attorney for the District of Columbia for presentation to the grand jury. The Attorney General directed the U.S. Attorney not to present the citation.

On March 10, 2008, the House Judiciary Committee initiated a civil suit seeking declaratory and injunctive relief to enforce the subpoenas. *Committee on the Judiciary v. Miers and Bolten*, Case No. 1:08 - cv-00409 (D.D.C.). The matter is currently pending before the district court.

End Notes

[1] See Archibald Cox, Executive Privilege, 122 U. of Pa. L. Rev. 1383, 1395-1405 (1979). See generally, Mark J. Rozelle, Executive Privilege: Presidential Powers, Secrecy, and Accountability, (2nd Edition, Revised 2002) (Rozelle); Mark J. Rozelle, Executive Privilege and Modern Presidents: In Nixon's Shadow, 83 Minn. L. Rev. 1069 (1999).
[2] See, Neil Devins, Congressional-Executive Information Access Disputes: A Modest Proposal-Do Nothing, 48 Adm. L.Rev. 109 (1996) (Devins).
[3] United States v. Nixon, 418 U.S. 683 (1974); Nixon v. Sirica, 487 F.2d 700 (D.C. Cir. 1973); Senate Select Committee v. Nixon, 498 F.2d 725 (D.C. Cir 1974); United States v. AT&T, 551 F.2d 384 (D.C. Cir. 1976), appeal after remand, 567 F.2d 121 (D.C. Cir. 1977); United States v. House of Representatives, 556 F.Supp. 150 (D.D.C. 1983); Espy , 121 F.3d 729 (D.C. Cir. 1997); In re Grand Jury Proceedings, 5 F. Supp. 2d 21 (D.D.C. 1998); Judicial Watch v. Department of Justice, 365 F. 3d 1108 (D. C. Cir. 2004).
[4] Senate Select Committee, supra; United States v. House of Representatives, supra; and United States v. AT&T, supra.
[5] Senate Select Committee, supra.
[6] Nixon v. Administrator of General Services, 433 U.S. 425 (1977).
[7] Judicial Watch, supra.
[8] 121 F.3d 729 (D.C. Cir. 1997).
[9] 365 F. 3d 1108 (D. C. Cir. 2004).
[10] 487 F.2d 750 (D.C. Cir. 1973).
[11] 487 F.2d at 717.
[12] Id.
[13] 498 F.2d 725 (D.C. Cir. 1974).
[14] 498 F.2d at 730-31.
[15] Id. at 731.
[16] Id. at 732 (emphasis supplied).
[17] Id. (emphasis supplied).
[18] Id. at 733.
[19] Id.
[20] This reading of Select Committee was a persistent characteristic of the statements of the Reagan, Bush and Clinton Administrations. See, e.g., Letter from Attorney General William French Smith to President Reagan, October 31, 1981, reprinted in 5 Op. OLC 27, 30 (1981) (Smith Letter/Watt); Memorandum to General Counsels' Consultative Group Re: Congressional Requests for Confidential Executive Branch Information, 13 Op. OLC 185, 192 (1989)(Barr Memo); letter from Attorney General Janet Reno to President Clinton, September 20, 1996, at 2-3 (Reno Letter/Haiti); Letter from Attorney General Janet Reno to President Clinton, September 16, 1999 (Reno/FALN). It is utilized in buttressing President George W. Bush's June 28, 2007, privilege claim with respect to demands for documents and testimony sought by the House and Senate Judiciary Committees relating to their investigations concerning the dismissal and replacement of nine U.S. Attorneys. See discussion supra at 24-26.

[21] 498 F. 2d at 731.
[22] Id. at 732-33.
[23] Id. at 733. It is important to note that the Select committee was established Senate Resolution 60 (1973) as a special investigation committee with no legislative authoirty. Its sole mission was to determine the facts about the Watergate break-in, and its aftermath, and report to the Senate its findings and recommendations.
[24] 2 The Records of the Constitutional Convention of 1787, at 206 (Max Farrand, ed., 1966).
[25] Woodrow Wilson, Congressional Government 195, 198 (Meridian Books 1956)(1885).
[26] See, e.g., Hutchinson v. Proxmire, 443 U.S. 111, 132 (1979).
[27] Watkins v. United States, 354 U.S. 173, 187 (1957). See also, McGrain v. Daugherty, U.S. 135, 177 (1926); Eastland v. U.S. Servicemen's Fund, 421 U.S. 491, 504 n. 15 (1975).
[28] 418 U.S. 683 (1974)(Nixon I).
[29] 418 U.S. 705, 706. See also, id. at 708, 711.
[30] Id. at 705, 706, 708.
[31] Id. at 706.
[32] Id.
[33] Id. at 707.
[34] Id. at 713.
[35] Id. at 712 n. 19.
[36] 433 U.S. 425 (1977)(Nixon II).
[37] Id. at 439.
[38] Id. at 446.
[39] Id. at 449 (citations omitted).
[40] Id. at 453.
[41] 567 F.2d 121 (D.C. Cir. 1977).
[42] This was the second time the case was before the court. After its initial review it was remanded to the district court to allow the parties further opportunity to negotiate an accommodation. See 551 F.2d 384 (D.C. Cir. 1976).
[43] Id. at 127 n.17.
[44] Id. at 128.
[45] Id. at 128.
[46] Id. at 129.
[47] Id. at 127-28.
[48] Id. at 127 (footnote omitted).]
[49] Id. at 130.
[50] Id. at 123, 126.
[51] Id. at 131-32.
[52] 556 F.Supp. 150 (D.D.C. 1983).
[53] Id. at 151.
[54] Id. at 152.
[55] Id. at 153.
[56] Id. at 152, 153.
[57] See Devins, supra, n. 2 at 118-120.
[58] See Smith letter, supra note 20; 5 Op. OLC at 28-31; Barr Memo, supra n.20; 13 Op. OLC at 187-190; Reno/FALN letter, supra n. 20.
[59] See, e.g., 418 U.S. at 705. See also, Smith Letter, supra, note 20, 5 Op. OLC at 29; Memorandum for All Executive Department and Agency General Counsel's Re: Congressional Requests to Departments and Agencies Protected By Executive Privilege, September 28, 1994, at 1, 2 (Cutler Memo); Letter from Jack Quinn to Hon. William A. Zellif, Jr., October 1, 1996, at 1 (Quinn Letter/FBI); Memorandum from President Bush to Secretary of Defense Richard Cheney Re: Congressional Subpoena for an Executive Branch Document, August 8, 1991, at 1 (Bush Memo).

60 Smith Letter/Watt, supra n. 20 at 31; see also id. at 30 ("congressional oversight interest will support a demand for predecisional, deliberative documents in the possession of the Executive Branch only in the most unusual circumstances"). Accord, Barr Memo, supra n.20 at 192 ("Congress will seldom have any legitimate legislative interest in knowing the precise predecisional positions and statements of particular Executive Branch officials".); letter from Assistant Attorney General Robert Rabkin, Office of Legislative Affairs, DOJ, to Honorable John Linder, Chairman House Subcommittee on Rules and Organization of the House, Committee on Rules, June 27, 2000 at 5-6 (Rabkin Letter)("[T]he Departmen has a broad confidentiality interest in matters that reflect its internal deliberative process. In particular, we have sought to ensure that all law enforcement and litigation decisions are products of open, frank, and independent assessments of the law and facts — uninhibited by political and improper influences that may be present outside the department. We have long been concerned about the chilling effect that would ripple throughout government if prosecutors, policy advisors at all levels and line attorneys believed that their honest opinion — be it 'good' or 'bad' - may be the topic of debate in Congressional hearings or floor debates. These include assessments of evidence and law, candid advice on strength and weaknesses of legal arguments, and recommendations to take or not to take legal action against individuals and corporate entities.").

61 Smith Letter/Watt, supra n. 20 at 30; see also Statement of Assistant Attorney General William H. Rehnquist, reprinted in Executive Privilege: The Withholding of Information by the Executive: Hearings Before the Subcommittee on Separation of Powers of the Senate Committee on the Judiciary, 92d Cong. 1st Sess. 424 (Rehnquist Statement). ("The notion that the advisors whom he has chosen should bear some sort of a hybrid responsibility to opinion makers outside of the government, which notion in practice would inevitably have the effect of diluting their responsibility to him, is entirely inconsistent with our tripartite systems of government. The President is entitled to undivided and faithful advice from his subordinates, just as Senators and Representatives are entitled to the same sort of advice from their legislative and administrative assistants, and judges to the same sort of advice from their law clerks."); Rabkin Letter *id.* at n.60 ("The foregoing concerns apply with special force to Congressional requests for prosecution and declination memoranda and similar documents. These are extremely sensitive law enforcement materials. The Department's attorneys are asked to render unbiased, professional judgments about the merits of potential criminal and civil law enforcement cases. If their deliberative documents were made subject to Congressional challenge and scrutiny, we would face a grave danger that they would be chilled from providing the candid and independent analysis essential to just and effective law enforcement or just as troubling, that our assessments of the strengths and weaknesses of evidence of the law, before they are presented in court. That may result in an unfair advantage to those who seek public funds and deprive the taxpayers of confidential representation enjoyed by other litigants.").

62 Smith Letter/Watt, supra n. 20; 5 Op. OLC at 29.

63 See Rozell, supra n.1 at 39 - 40.

64 In his prepared statement to the Subcommittee on Separation of Powers of the Senate Judiciary Committee, Assistant Attorney General Rehnquist distinguished between "those few executive branch witnesses whose sole responsibility is that of advising the President" who "should not be required to appear [before Congress] at all, since all of their official responsibilities would be subject to a claim of privilege" and "the executive branch witness ... whose responsibilities include the administration of departments or agencies established by Congress, and from whom Congress may quite properly require extensive testimony," subject to "appropriate" claims of privilege. Rehnquist Statement, supra n. 10 at 427. Moreover, in colloquy with Senator Helms, Mr. Rehnquist seemed to accept that the privilege protected only communications with some nexus to presidential decisionmaking:
SENATOR ERVIN: As I construe your testimony, the decisionmaking process category would apply to communications between presidential advisers and the President and also to

communications made between subordinates of the President when they are engaged in the process of determining what recommendations they should make to the President in respect to matters of policy.

MR. REHNQUIST: It would certainly extend that far, yes.

Id. at 439-40. See also Roelle, supra n.1 at 65-66.

[65] See Memorandum for the Attorney General Re: Confidentiality of the Attorney General's Communications in Counseling the President, 6 Op. OLC 481, 489 (1982)(Olson Memo).

[66] Bush Memo, supra n. 59 at 1. Letter from General Counsel, DOD, Terrence O'Donnell to Hon. John Conyers, Jr., October 8, 1991, at 5 (O'Donnell Letter).

[67] See, e.g., Cutler Memo, supra n. 59 at 2.

[68] See, e.g., Cutler Memo, supra n. 59 at 2 (Communications between White House and departments or agencies, including advice to or from to White House); Reno/FALN letter, supra n. 20.

[69] *See Presidential Signing Statements: Constitutional and Institutional Implications*, CRS Report RL33667 by T.J. Halstead, September 20, 2006.

[70] See e.g., Executive Order 13233 issued by President Bush on November 1, 2001, which gave current and former presidents and vice presidents broad authority to withhold presidential records and delay their release indefinitely. It vests former vice presidents, and the heirs or designees of disabled or deceased presidents the authority to assert executive privilege, and expands the scope of claims of privilege. Hearings held by the House Committee on Government Reform in 2002 raised substantial questions as to the constitutionality of the Order and resulted in the reporting of legislation (H.R. 4187) in the 107th Congress that would have nullified the Order and established new processes for presidential claims of privilege and for congressional and public access to presidential records. H.Rept. No. 107-790, 107th Cong. 2nd Sess. (2002). Substantially the same legislation (H.R. 1225) passed the House on March 14, 2007. See H.Rept. 110-44, 110th Cong. 1st Sess. (2007), and was reported out of the Senate Committee on Homeland Security and Governmental Affairs on June 20, 2007, without amendment and with no written report. See generally, Jonathan Turley, "Presidential Papers and Popular Government: The Convergence of Constitutional and Property Theory in Claims of Ownership and Control of Presidential Records." 88 Cornell L. Rev. 651, 666-696 (2003).

[71] *See* Letter dated May 21, 2004 to Hon. Alex M. Azar, II, General Counsel, Department of Health and Human Services from Jack L. Goldsmith III, Assistant Attorney General, Office of Legal Counsel, Department of Justice, *available at,* [http://www.usdoj.gov/olc/crsmemoresponsese.html]

[72] Id.. at 3.

[73] Cutler Memo, supra n. 59 at 1.

[74] Congressional Subpoenas of Department of Justice Investigative Files, 8 Op. OLC 315 (1984). Accord, Smith Letter/EPA, supra n. 20 at 36 ("These principles will not be employed to shield documents which contain evidence of criminal or unethical conduct by agency officials from proper review".).

[75] See David Hoffman, "President Offers to Share Iran Sales Notes with Hill; Aides Reversed on Memoir Materials." *Washington Post*, February 3, 1987, at A1.

[76] Olson Memo, supra n. 64 at 486; Rabkin Letter, supra n. 60.

[77] Id.; but see Smith Letter/EPA, supra n. 20 at 32 ("policy does not extend to all material contained in investigative files .... The only documents which have been withheld are those which are sensitive memoranda or notes by ... attorneys and investigators reflecting enforcement strategy, legal analysis, lists of potential witnesses, settlement considerations, and similar materials the disclosure of which might adversely affect a pending enforcement action, overall enforcement policy, or the rights of individuals".).

[78] Cutler Memo, supra n. 59 at 1. Accord Memorandum from President Reagan for the Heads of Executive Departments, and Agencies Re: Procedures for Governing Responses to

Congressional Requests for Information, November 4, 1982 (Reagan Memo); Rabkin Letter, supra n. 60, at 1-2

[79] Cutler Memo, supra n. 59 at 1.

[80] Reagan Memo, supra n. 74, at 1.

[81] Barr Memo, supra n. 20, at 185.

[82] Id. at 185, 186. See Rozelle supra n.1 at 106-108.

[83] Rehnquist Statement, supra n. 63, at 420.

[84] Smith Letter/Watt, supra n. 20, at 31.

[85] Reagan Memo, supra n. 74, at 1.

[86] Rehnquist Statement, supra n. 63, at 422.

[87] Id.

[88] Letter from Attorney General Janet Reno to President Clinton, September 20, 1996, at 2-3 (Reno Letter/Haiti); letter from Attorney General Reno to President Clinton, September 30, 1996, at 2 (Reno Letter/FBI); letter from Attorney General Reno to President Clinton, September 16, 1999 (Reno Letter/FALN). The Acting Attorney General's opinion accompanying President George W. Bush's June 28, 2007, claim of executive privilege, discussed in infra at 24-26, relies heavily on the Senate Select Committee precedent.

[89] 498 F.2d at 731.

[90] Cutler Memo, supra n. 20 at 2-3.

[91] Reagan Memo, supra n. 71 at 2.

[92] See the Appendix of this Report for a compilation of executive privilege claims from the Kennedy through the George W. Bush Administrations.

[93] Clinton v. Jones, 520 U.S. 681(1997)(no temporary presidential immunity from civil suit for unofficial acts); In re Grand Jury Subpoena Duces Tecum, 112 F.3d 910 (8th Cir. 1997), cert. denied 521 U.S. 1105 (1997)(claims of attorney-client and work product privilege denied); In re Sealed Case, 121 F.3d 729 (D.C. Cir 1977)(claims of executive privilege rejected); In re Sealed Case, 124 F.3d 230 (D.C. Cir. 1997)(claims of attorney-client and work product privilege denied); In re Sealed Case, 148 F. 3d 1073 (D.C. Cir.) cert. denied 525 U.S.990(1998) (claim of "protective function" privilege denied); In re Bruce R. Lindsey (Grand Jury Testimony), 148 F. 3d 1100 (D.C. Cir. 1998) (claims of attorney-client and work product privilege denied).

[94] 121 F.3d 729 (D.C. Cir. 1997).

[95] 121 F.3d at 745, 746; see also id. at 737-738 ("[W]here there is reason to believe the documents sought may shed light on government misconduct, the [deliberative process] privilege is routinely denied on the grounds that shielding internal government deliberations in this context does not serve 'the public interest in honest, effective government'").

[96] Id. at 745, 752. See also id. at 753 ("... these communications nonetheless are connected with presidential decisionmaking").

[97] Id. at 754. See also id. at 757.

[98] In contrast, the deliberative process privilege does not protect documents that simply state or explain a decision the government has already made or material that is purely factual, unless the material is inextricably intertwined with the deliberative portions of the materials so that disclosure would effectively reveal the deliberations. 121 F.3d at 737.

[99] Id. at 745.

[100] Id. at 752.

[101] Id.

[102] Id. (footnote omitted).

[103] Id. at 752.

[104] Id. at 752-53.

[105] See, e.g., Kendall ex rel. Stokes v. United States, 37 U.S. (12 Pet.) 522, 612-613 (1838); Youngstown Sheet & Tube Co. v. Sawyer, 343 U.S. 579, 587 (1952); Myers v. United States, 272 U.S. 52, 177 (1926)(Holmes, J., dissenting); National Treasury Employees Union v. Nixon, 492 F.2d 587, 604 (D.C. Cir. 1974).

[106] 121 F.3d at 748.
[107] Id. at 750.
[108] Id. at 752.
[109] 365 F.3d 1108 (D.C. Cir. 2004). The panel split 2-1, with Judge Rogers writing for the majority and Judge Randolph dissenting.
[110] The President has delegated the formal process of review and recommendation of his pardon authority to the Attorney General who, in turn, has delegated it to the Deputy Attorney General. The Deputy Attorney General oversees the work of the Office of the Pardon Attorney.
[111] 365 F.3d at 1109-12.
[112] *Id.* at 1112, 1114, 1123.
[113] *Id.* at 1114.
[114] *Id.* at 1117.
[115] *Id.* at 1121-22.
[116] *Id.* at 1116.
[117] *Id.* at 1116-117.
[118] *Id.* at 1118-24.
[119] 16 U.S.C. 431 (2000).
[120] See 143 Cong. Rec. E2259-2272 (daily ed. November 9, 1997)(Remarks of Hon. James V. Hansen presenting staff study of committee actions and documents in regard to the establishment of the Grand Staircase-Escalante National Monument). See also Ruth Larson, "White House Yields Papers on Utah Wilderness Decision," *Wash. Times*, October 23, 1997, A3. Of course, the White House action cannot be deemed a concession of the legal argument in the absence of an explanation for its decision to disclose the material.
[121] The notion that a congressional delegation of administrative decisionmaking authority is implicitly a concurrent delegation of authority to the President, is effectively countered by Professor Kevin Stack in "The President's Statutory Power to Administer the Laws," 106 Colum. L. Rev. 263 (2006).
[122] Letter dated June 28, 2007 to Chairman Conyers and Leahy from Fred F. Fielding, Counsel to the President.
[123] Memorandum, dated June 27, 2007, for the President from Paul D. Clement, Solicitor General and Acting Attorney General (Clement Memo).
[124] Clement Memo at 1.
[125] Clement Memo at 2.
[126] Id. at 3.
[127] Id at 5-6.
[128] Id. at 6.
[129] Id. at 6-7.
[130] "Memorandum for the Counsel to the President Re: Immunity of Former Counsel to the President from Compelled Congressional Testimony" from Principal Deputy Assistant Attorney General, Office Legal Counsel, DOJ, dated July 10, 2007 (OLC Immunity Opinion).
[131] H.Rept. No. 110-423 110th Cong., 1st Sess. (2007).
[132] H.Res. 979, 110th Cong. (February 14, 2008).
[133] *Committee on the Judiciary, United States House of Representatives* v. *Harriet Miers and Joshua Bolten*, Case No. 1:08-er-00409 (D.D.C.) (JDB).
[134] See Appendix.
[135] See, "Everything Secret Degenerates: The FBI's Use of Murderers and Informants," H.Rept. No. 108-414, 108th Cong. 2nd Sess. 121-134 (2004).
[136] 418 U.S. 683, 708 (1974).
[137] See, *e.g.*, *Nixon* v. *Administrator of General Services*, 433 U.S. 425, 446-471 (1977); *United States* v. *AT&T*, 567 F. 2d. 121,178 (D.C. Cir. 1977); *In re Sealed Case (Espy),* 121 F. 3d. 729, 744-46, 753-57 (D.C. Cir. 1997). See also *In Re Bruce Lindsey*, 158 F. 3d 1263,

1266,1278 (D.C. Cir.1998) (rejecting a claim of absolute immunity for attorney-client communication in the face of a grand jury subpoena by a White House counsel on the ground, *inter alia*, that such a claim, if accepted, would provide more protection than would be afforded by a qualified claim of presidential privilege).

[138] See footnote 130, *supra*, and accompanying text.

In: Presidental Advisers and Claims… ISBN: 978-1-60692-552-2
Editors: William A. Galvan

Chapter 2

PRESIDENTIAL ADVISERS' TESTIMONY BEFORE CONGRESSIONAL COMMITTEES: AN OVERVIEW

Harold C. Relyea and Todd B. Tatelman

SUMMARY

Since the beginning of the federal government, Presidents have called upon executive branch officials to provide them with advice regarding matters of policy and administration. While Cabinet members were among the first to play such a role, the creation of the Executive Office of the President (EOP) in 1939 and the various agencies located within that structure resulted in a large increase in the number and variety of presidential advisers. All senior staff members of the White House Office and the leaders of the various EOP agencies and instrumentalities could be said to serve as advisers to the President.

Occasionally, these executive branch officials playing a presidential advisory role have been called upon to testify before congressional committees and subcommittees. Sometimes, such invited appearances have been prompted by allegations of personal misconduct on the part of the official, but they have also included instances when accountability for policymaking and administrative or managerial actions have instigated the request for testimony. Because such appearances before congressional committees or subcommittees seemingly could result in demands for advice proffered to the President, or the disclosure — inadvertent or otherwise — of such advice, there has been resistance, from time to time, by the Chief Executive to allowing such testimony.

Congress has a constitutionally rooted right of access to the information it needs to perform its Article I legislative and oversight functions. Generally, a congressional committee with jurisdiction over the subject matter, which is conducting an authorized investigation for legislative or oversight purposes, has a right to information held by the executive branch in the absence of either a valid claim of constitutional privilege by the executive or a statutory provision whereby Congress has limited its constitutional right to information.

A congressional committee may request (informally or by a letter from the committee chair, perhaps co-signed by the ranking Member) or demand (pursuant to subpoena) the testimony of a presidential adviser. However, Congress may encounter legal and political problems in attempting to enforce a subpoena to a presidential adviser. Conflicts concerning congressional requests or demands for executive branch testimony or documents often involve extensive negotiations and may be resolved by some form of compromise as to, inter alia, the scope of the testimony or information to be provided to Congress.

(Note: This report was originally co-authored by Jay R. Shampansky, Legislative Attorney.)

Since the beginning of the federal government, Presidents have called upon executive branch officials to provide them with advice regarding matters of policy and administration. The Constitution recognized such relationships when it authorized the President, in Article II, Section 2, to "require the Opinion, in writing, of the principal Officer in each of the executive Departments, upon any Subject relating to the Duties of their respective Offices." There were, as well, reasons to expect that such advice, whether offered orally or in writing, would be held in confidence. The advice was for the President's consideration and his decisionmaking. The matters involved were sensitive, perhaps bearing upon the foreign, military, economic, or law enforcement policy of the nation. Also, the provision, discussion, and use of such advice by the executive branch could affect its relationships with the other coequal constitutional branches. President George Washington and his Cabinet had these considerations in mind, as Secretary of State Thomas Jefferson's notes on their deliberations reflect, when they decided upon a response to a 1792 congressional request for information.

> We had all considered, and were of one mind, first, that the House was an inquest, and therefore might institute inquiries. Second that it

> might call for papers generally. Third, that the Executive ought to communicate such papers as the public good would permit, and ought to refuse those, the disclosure of which would injure the public; consequently were to exercise a discretion. Fourth, that neither the committee nor House had a right to call on the Head of a Department, who and whose papers were under the President alone; but that the committee should instruct their chairman to move the House to address the President....[1]

The Cabinet, composed of the principal officers in each of the executive departments, failed, for several reasons, to develop as an important source of presidential advice. The department heads constituting the Cabinet were often chosen to satisfy interests that contributed significantly to the President's election. Considerations of partisanship, ideology, geography, public image and stature, and aptitude, among others, figured prominently in their selection. Sometimes the President was not personally well acquainted with these individuals and had only minimal confidence and trust in them. In a few cases, a political rival was included in the Cabinet.

It is also very likely that some activist Presidents were ill suited to the group deliberation of the Cabinet. Similarly, many Cabinet members might have felt unqualified, or were unwilling, to offer counsel to the President on matters outside of their immediate portfolios; their advice was perhaps limited to, and protective of, departmental interests. Finally, personal hostilities between or among department heads could result in such tumult within the Cabinet that little useful advice could be gained.

Consequently, Presidents generally looked to other quarters for advisers. One development in this regard was the creation of circles of advisers composed of both public officials and private citizens. President Andrew Jackson, whose election and White House tenure occurred in an era marked by violent political controversy and party instability, utilized an informal group of advisers which came to be known as the Kitchen Cabinet. The members represented "rising social groups as yet denied the prestige to which they felt their power and energies entitled them" — newspapermen, the President's private secretary, campaign organizers and officials from prior administrations, and longtime personal friends.[2]

When John Tyler succeeded to the presidency upon the death of William Henry Harrison, he revived Jackson's practice. Deserted by Whigs and Democrats alike, Tyler resorted to a select circle of advisers composed of personal and political friends from his native Virginia — a college president, a state supreme court judge, four members of the state's delegation in the House of Representatives, and a Senator.[3] Following this practice, several succeeding Presidents had informal groups of advisers that were given colorful names by the press. For example, for Grover Cleveland, it was a Fishing Cabinet; for Theodore Roosevelt, a Tennis Cabinet; for Warren G. Harding, a Poker Cabinet; and for Herbert Hoover, a Medicine Ball Cabinet.

Jackson's inclusion of his personal secretary in his Kitchen Cabinet reflects another line of development regarding presidential advisers. Beginning with Washington, Presidents sought to meet the demands of their office with the assistance of a single personal secretary, usually a relative, compensated from their own private resources. In 1833, Congress authorized the President to appoint, with the advise and consent of the Senate, a secretary "whose duty it shall be, under the direction of the President, to sign in his name and for him, all patents for lands sold or granted under the authority of the United States."[4] Jackson named Andrew Jackson Donelson, his wife's nephew and current personal secretary, to this position, relieving himself of continued personal compensation of the young man. Ultimately, Congress appropriated funds to the Chief Executive in 1857 for an official household — a personal secretary, a steward to supervise the Executive Mansion, and a messenger[5].

Many years later, in 1929, Congress was persuaded to authorize an increase in the President's top personnel, adding two more secretaries and an administrative assistant.[6] Appointed to these senior staff positions were presidential lieutenants, if not presidential intimates and advisers. When Franklin D. Roosevelt came to the presidency in 1933, he brought with him, from his New York gubernatorial experience, a new kind of advisory circle, composed of intellectuals, or at least a core group of Columbia University professors who were joined by other ideas people to form the "Brains Trust." Because there were an insufficient number of staff positions at the White House to accommodate them, these advisers were placed elsewhere in the executive branch, but, for the most part, directly served the President.[7]

This staffing situation, coordination problems, and the development of a new administrative management concept prompted Roosevelt to create, by announcement, a study panel — the President's Committee on Administrative Management, under the leadership of Louis Brownlow, a prominent public administration practitioner — in 1936 to examine and make recommendations regarding these matters.[8] Reporting some 10 months later, the Brownlow committee addressed presidential staffing in dramatic and detailed terms.

> The President needs help. His immediate staff assistance is entirely inadequate. He should be given a small number of executive assistants who would be his direct aides in dealing with the managerial agencies and administrative departments of the government. These assistants, probably not exceeding six in number, would be in addition to the present secretaries, who deal with the public, with the Congress, and with the press and radio. These aides would have no power to make decisions or issue instructions in their own right. They would not be interposed between the President and the heads of his departments. They would not be assistant presidents in any sense. Their function would be, when any matter was presented to the President for action affecting any part of the administrative work of the Government, to assist him in obtaining quickly and without delay all pertinent information possessed by any of the executive departments so as to guide him in making his responsible decisions; and then when decisions have been made, to assist him in seeing to it that every administrative department and agency affected is promptly informed. Their effectiveness in assisting the President will, we think, be directly proportional to their ability to discharge their functions with restraint. They would remain in the background, issue no orders, make no decisions, emit no public statements. Men for these positions should be carefully chosen by the President from within and without the Government. They should be men in whom the President has personal confidence and whose character and attitude is [sic] such that they would not attempt to exercise power on their own account. They should be possessed of high competence, great physical vigor, and a passion for anonymity. They should be installed in the White House itself, directly accessible to the President. In the selection of these aides, the President should be free to call on departments from time to time for the assignment of persons who, after a tour of duty as his aides, might be restored to their old positions.[9]

In addition to the proposed addition of six assistants to the President's staff, the committee's report also recommended vesting responsibility in the President for the continuous reorganization of the executive branch. Released to Congress on January 12, 1937, the report soon became lost in high politics. Three weeks after submitting the Brownlow committee's report to Congress, Roosevelt announced he wanted to enlarge the membership of the Supreme Court. His "court packing" plan not only fed congressional fears of a presidential power grab, but also so preoccupied Congress that the Brownlow committee's recommendations were ignored.

EXECUTIVE OFFICE OF THE PRESIDENT

Although efforts at gaining legislative approval of the Brownlow committee's recommendations lay in ruin in the spring of 1938, the President had not deserted the cause. By July, Roosevelt was meeting with Brownlow and the other committee members. The panel would not be officially reassembled, but he wanted each man's help with a reorganization authority proposal. The resulting measure empowered the President to propose reorganization plans, subject to a veto by a majority vote of disapproval in both houses of Congress, and to also appoint six administrative assistants.

After three days of discussion and debate, the House adopted the bill on March 8, 1939. Twelve days later, the Senate began considering the proposal. Following two days of sparring over amendments, the Senate adopted the bill. A quick conference cleared the measure for Roosevelt's signature on April 3.[10] Earlier, the President had asked the Brownlow committee members to assist with the preparation of his initial reorganization plans.[11]

Following consultations with Budget Bureau Director Harold D. Smith, the Brownlow group presented two reorganization proposals to Roosevelt on April 23. Plan 1, submitted to Congress on April 25, transferred certain agencies to the Executive Office of the President, but offered no explanation of that entity.[12] In Plan 2, a presidential emergency council was abolished and most of its functions were transferred to the Executive Office.[13] While both plans were acceptable to legislators, their effective dates were troublesome in terms of accommodating fiscal calendar necessities. By joint resolution, Congress provided that both plans would be effective on July 1, 1939.[14] Following this action, the President, on September 8, issued E.O. 8248, formally organizing the Executive Office and, thereby, defining it in terms of its components.[15] Brownlow, who drafted the initial reorganization plan, viewed the Executive Office as the institutional realization of administrative management and "the effective coordination of the tremendously wide-spread federal machinery." He called the initial version "a little thing" compared to its later size. It grew under Roosevelt and "it continued to expand and was further regularized by statute, by appropriation acts, and by more reorganization plans" during the succeeding years.[16]

The Executive Office organized by E.O. 8248 consisted of the White House Office, the Bureau of the Budget, the National Resources Planning Board, the Office of Government Reports, and the Liaison Office for Personnel Management. It also provided that, "in the event of a national emergency," there could be established "such office for emergency management as the President shall determine." The Office for Emergency Management was created by an administrative order on May 25, 1940, and its functions were further specified in an administrative order of January 7, 1941.[17] It subsequently served as a parent unit for a number of subordinate emergency management bodies.

Presidential Adviser Growth

The creation of the Executive Office of the President contributed to an increase in the number of presidential advisers for several reasons. First, it provided an enclave for various agencies that immediately assisted the President. Primary among these was the White House Office, which was no longer merely the President's small office staff, but an agency with hierarchically organized staff positions whose personnel rapidly expanded during the next few decades.

Second, it counted agencies, such as the Liaison Office for Personnel Management and the Office for Emergency Management, that were headed by an administrative assistant — and adviser — to the President on the White House Office payroll. It also included agencies, such as the Bureau of the Budget (and its Office of Management and Budget successor), that were headed by leaders for whom advising the President was a primary responsibility.

Third, senior White House Office staff would come to supervise and direct the staff of other Executive Office entities: the Assistant to the President for National Security Affairs would direct the National Security Council staff and the Assistant to the President for Domestic Policy would direct the Domestic Council staff.

Fourth, in January 1973, President Richard M. Nixon vested his Secretary of the Treasury and his director of the Office of Management and Budget with dual White House Office positions, respectively, of Assistant to the President for Economic Affairs and Assistant to the President for Executive Management. He also vested his Secretary of Agriculture, Secretary of Health, Education, and Welfare, and Secretary of Housing and Urban Development with dual White House Office positions, respectively, of Counselor to the President for Natural Resources, Counselor to the President for Human Resources, and Counselor to the President for Community Development.[18] Having such dual White House Office titles was viewed as giving added emphasis, if not authority, to the role of these officials as presidential advisers.

In the aftermath of World War II, Congress statutorily chartered most of the agencies within the Executive Office of the President. Furthermore, Congress routinely appropriated funds for the operating expenses of these entities. In 1944, Congress had adopted an amendment to an appropriation bill that was designed to restrain the creation of Executive Office agencies by executive order — a frequent occurrence during 1941-1944. The amendment stated:

> After January 1, 1945, no part of any appropriation or fund made available by this or any other Act shall be allotted or made available to, or used to pay the expenses of, any agency or instrumentality including those established by Executive order after such agency or instrumentality has been in existence for more than one year, if the Congress has not appropriated any money specifically for such agency or instrumentality or specifically authorized the expenditure of funds by it.[19]

In 1982, when Title 31 of the United States Code was recodified, the amendment was repealed and replaced with new language at Section 1347.[20] The opening sentence of the new section, which remains as operative law, states: "An agency in existence for more than one year may not use amounts otherwise available for obligation to pay its expenses without a specific appropriation or specific authorization by law."

With their growing number and influence, senior staff members of the White House Office and certain other Executive Office agencies began to become of interest to congressional committees when accountability for policymaking and administrative or managerial actions prompted requests for their testimony. Some, like War Production Board chairman Donald M. Nelson,[21] who was popularly known as the "arms czar," appeared before and cooperated with the Senate Special Committee to Investigate the National Defense Program ("Truman Committee") during World War II to report on and discuss war material production and related coordination matters.[22] Others, like Office of War Mobilization director James F. Byrnes, who was sometimes referred to as the "assistant president," apparently avoided appearing before congressional committees during the World War II era, but were in communication with various individual Members of Congress in leadership positions and served as liaisons between the President and Congress on a number of war matters.[23]

Presidential Adviser Testimony

Beginning with the closing years of World War II, examples are provided below of instances when a presidential adviser — a civilian executive branch official, other than a member of the traditional Cabinet, who, as part of that official's responsibilities and activities, consulted with the President — testified before a congressional committee or subcommittee. Because these consultations with the President by such an official may be considered by the President to be privileged and constitutionally protectable, examples are also provided of instances when invited congressional committee or subcommittee testimony by a presidential adviser was refused. None of the examples involves testimony or refusal to testify by a former presidential adviser. All examples are based upon the public record.

- Jonathan Daniels, Administrative Assistant to the President, White House Office, appeared before the Senate Committee on Agriculture and Forestry on February 28 and March 7 and 8, 1944, to discuss his involvement in the personnel policy of the Rural Electrification Administration.[24]
- Wallace H. Graham, Physician to the President, White House Office, appeared before the Senate Committee on Appropriations on January 13, 1948, to discuss information to which he might have been privy with regard to the commodity market.[25]
- Harry H. Vaughn, Military Aide to the President, White House Office, appeared before the Senate Committee on Expenditures in Executive Departments (now Governmental Affairs) on August 30 and 31, 1949, to discuss his personal involvement in certain government procurement contracts.[26]
- Donald S. Dawson, Administrative Assistant to the President, White House Office, appeared before the Senate Committee on Banking and Currency on May 10 and 11, 1951, to discuss allegations he had attempted to "dominate" the Reconstruction Finance Corporation and influence appointments to that body.[27]
- Sherman Adams, Assistant to the President, White House Office, appeared before the House Committee on Interstate and Foreign Commerce Committee on June 17, 1958, to discuss his involvement with certain lobbyists.[28]
- Edward E. David, Jr., Science Adviser to the President, White House Office, and director, Office of Science and Technology, appeared

before the Senate Committee on Interior and Insular Affairs on June 15, 1971, to discuss the Nixon Administration's position on energy policy matters; he appeared again before the House Committee on Science and Astronautics on June 14, 1972, to discuss science policy matters relating to Soviet-American cooperation agreements.[29]

- Virginia H. Knauer, Special Assistant to the President for Consumer Affairs, White House Office, and director, Office of Consumer Affairs, appeared before the House Select Committee on Small Business on June 25, 1971, to discuss consumer protection and advertising standards.[30]
- Jerome H. Jaffe, Special Consultant to the President, White House Office, and director, Special Action Office for Drug Abuse Prevention, appeared before the House Committee on Interstate and Foreign Commerce on June 28, August 2, October 27, and November 8, 1971, to discuss various aspects of the operations of the Special Action Office.[31]
- Peter Flanigan, Assistant to the President, White House Office, appeared before the Senate Committee on the Judiciary on April 20, 1972, during the course of hearings on the confirmation of Richard Kleindienst as Attorney General to discuss his involvement in apparent lobbying activities by the International Telephone and Telegraph Company.[32]
- Bruce A. Kehrli, Special Assistant to the President, White House Office, appeared before the Senate Select Committee on Presidential Campaign Activities on May 17, 1973, to discuss matters related to the Watergate incident.[33]
- Patrick J. Buchanan, Special Consultant to the President, White House Office, appeared before the Senate Select Committee on Presidential Campaign Activities on September 26, 1973, to discuss matters related to the Watergate incident.[34]
- Richard M. Harden, Special Assistant to the President, White House Office, appeared before the Senate Appropriations Subcommittee on Treasury, Postal Service, and General Government on March 9, 1977, to discuss funds for the White House Office; he appeared again before the House Appropriations Subcommittee on Treasury, Postal Service, and General Government on March 15, 1977, to discuss these same matters.[35]
- Rose Mary Woods, Personal Secretary to the President, White House Office, appeared before the Senate Select Committee on Presidential

Campaign Activities on March 22, 1974, to discuss matters related to the Watergate incident.[36]

- J. Frederick Buzhardt, Special Counsel to the President, White House Office, appeared before the Senate Select Committee on Presidential Campaign Activities on April 10 and May 7, 1974, to discuss matters related to the Watergate incident.[37]
- Alexander M. Haig, Jr., Staff Coordinator to the President, White House Office, appeared before the Senate Select Committee on Presidential Campaign Activities on May 2, and 15, 1974, to discuss matters related to the Watergate incident.[38]
- Leonard Garment, Assistant to the President, White House Office, appeared before the Senate Select Committee on Presidential Campaign Activities on May 17, 1974, to discuss matters related to the Watergate incident.[39]
- Lloyd Cutler, Counsel to the President, White House Office, appeared before the Senate Judiciary Subcommittee to Investigate the Activities of Individuals Representing the Interests of Foreign Governments on September 10, 1980, to discuss efforts by the President's brother, Billy Carter, to influence the federal government on behalf of the government of Libya.[40]
- Zbigniew Brzezinski, Assistant to the President for National Security Affairs, White House Office, appeared before the Senate Judiciary Subcommittee to Investigate the Activities of Individuals Representing the Interests of Foreign Governments on September 17, 1980, to discuss efforts by the President's brother, Billy Carter, to influence the federal government on behalf of the government of Libya.[41]
- Samuel Berger, Deputy Assistant to the President for National Security Affairs, White House Office, appeared before the Senate Committee on Foreign Relations on May 3, 1994, to provide a briefing on United States policy toward Haiti.[42]
- Samuel Berger, Assistant to the President for National Security Affairs, White House Office, appeared before the Senate Committee on Governmental Affairs on September 11, 1997, concerning campaign fund-raising practices in connection with the 1996 federal election campaign.[43]
- Lloyd N. Cutler, Special Counsel to the President, White House Office, appeared before the House Committee on Banking, Finance, and Urban Affairs on July 26, 1994, concerning whether White House

aides had inappropriately learned details of a Resolution Trust Corporation (RTC) investigation of the failed Madison Guaranty Savings and Loan.[44]

- Lisa M. Caputo, Press Secretary to the First Lady, White House Office, appeared before the House Committee on Banking, Finance, and Urban Affairs on July 28, 1994, concerning whether White House aides had inappropriately learned details of an RTC investigation of the failed Madison Guaranty Savings and Loan.[45]
- W. Neil Eggleston, Associate Counsel to the President, White House Office, appeared before the House Committee on Banking, Finance, and Urban Affairs on July 28, 1994, concerning whether White House aides had inappropriately learned details of an RTC investigation of the failed Madison Guaranty Savings and Loan.[46]
- Mark D. Gearan, Assistant to the President for Communications, appeared before the House Committee on Banking, Finance, and Urban Affairs on July 28, 1994, concerning whether White House aides had inappropriately learned details of an RTC investigation of the failed Madison Guaranty Savings and Loan.[47]
- Harold Ickes, Assistant to the President and Deputy Chief of Staff, White House Office, appeared before the House Committee on Banking, Finance, and Urban Affairs on July 28, 1994, concerning whether White House aides had inappropriately learned details of an RTC investigation of the failed Madison Guaranty Savings and Loan.[48]
- Bruce Lindsey, Assistant to the President and Senior Adviser, White House Office, appeared before the House Committee on Banking, Finance, and Urban Affairs on July 28, 1994, concerning whether White House aides had inappropriately learned details of an RTC investigation of the failed Madison Guaranty Savings and Loan.[49]
- John D. Podesta, Assistant to the President and Staff Secretary, White House Office, appeared before the House Committee on Banking, Finance, and Urban Affairs on July 28, 1994, concerning whether White House aides had inappropriately learned details of an RTC investigation of the failed Madison Guaranty Savings and Loan.[50]
- Clifford Sloan, Associate Counsel to the President, White House Office, appeared before the House Committee on Banking, Finance, and Urban Affairs on July 28, 1994, concerning whether White House aides had inappropriately learned details of an RTC investigation of the failed Madison Guaranty Savings and Loan.[51]

- George R. Stephanopoulos, Senior Policy adviser to the President, appeared before the House Committee on Banking, Finance, and Urban Affairs on July 28, 1994, concerning whether White House aides had inappropriately learned details of an RTC investigation of the failed Madison Guaranty Savings and Loan.[52]
- Margaret A. Williams, Chief of Staff to the First Lady, White House Office, appeared before the House Committee on Banking, Finance, and Urban Affairs on July 28, 1994, concerning whether White House aides had inappropriately learned details of an RTC investigation of the failed Madison Guaranty Savings and Loan.[53]
- Lloyd N. Cutler, Special Counsel to the President, White House Office, appeared before the Senate Committee on Banking, Housing, and Urban Affairs on August 5, 1994, concerning whether White House aides had inappropriately learned details of an RTC investigation of the failed Madison Guaranty Savings and Loan.[54]
- W. Neil Eggleston, Deputy Counsel to the President, White House Office, appeared before the Senate Committee on Banking, Housing, and Urban Affairs on August 3, 1994, concerning whether White House aides had inappropriately learned details of an RTC investigation of the failed Madison Guaranty Savings and Loan.[55]
- Harold Ickes, Assistant to the President and Deputy Chief of Staff, White House Office, appeared before the Senate Committee on Banking, Housing, and Urban Affairs on August 4, 1994, concerning whether White House aides had inappropriately learned details of an RTC investigation of the failed Madison Guaranty Savings and Loan.[56]
- Joel I. Klein, Deputy Counsel to the President, appeared before the Senate Committee on Banking, Housing, and Urban Affairs on August 3, 1994, concerning whether White House aides had inappropriately learned details of an RTC investigation of the failed Madison Guaranty Savings and Loan.[57]
- Bruce R. Lindsey, Assistant to the President and Senior Adviser, White House Office, appeared before the Senate Committee on Banking, Housing, and Urban Affairs on August 4, 1994, concerning whether White House aides had inappropriately learned details of an RTC investigation of the failed Madison Guaranty Savings and Loan.[58]
- Thomas F. McLarty III, Counselor to the President, White House Office, appeared before the Senate Committee on Banking, Housing,

and Urban Affairs on August 4, 1994, concerning whether White House aides had inappropriately learned details of an RTC investigation of the failed Madison Guaranty Savings and Loan.[59]

- Beth Nolan, Associate Counsel to the President, White House Office, appeared before the Senate Committee on Banking, Housing, and Urban Affairs on August 3, 1994, concerning whether White House aides had inappropriately learned details of an RTC investigation of the failed Madison Guaranty Savings and Loan.[60]
- John D. Podesta, Assistant to the President and Staff Secretary, White House Office, appeared before the Senate Committee on Banking, Housing, and Urban Affairs on August 4, 1994, concerning whether White House aides had inappropriately learned details of an RTC investigation of the failed Madison Guaranty Savings and Loan.[61]
- Clifford M. Sloan, Associate Counsel to the President, White House Office, appeared before the Senate Committee on Banking, Housing, and Urban Affairs on August 3, 1994, concerning whether White House aides had inappropriately learned details of an RTC investigation of the failed Madison Guaranty Savings and Loan.[62]
- George R. Stephanopoulos, Senior Adviser to the President for Policy and Strategy, White House Office, appeared before the Senate Committee on Banking, Housing, and Urban Affairs on August 4, 1994, concerning whether White House aides had inappropriately learned details of an RTC investigation of the failed Madison Guaranty Savings and Loan.[63]
- Margaret A. Williams, Assistant to the President and Chief of Staff to the First Lady, White House Office, appeared before the Senate Committee on Banking, Housing, and Urban Affairs on August 4, 1994, concerning whether White House aides had inappropriately learned details of an RTC investigation of the failed Madison Guaranty Savings and Loan.[64]
- Mark D. Gearan, Assistant to the President and Director of Communications and Strategic Planning, White House Office, appeared before the Senate Special Committee to Investigate the Whitewater Development Corporation and Related Matters on July 25, 1995, concerning whether White House staff had engaged in improper contacts regarding the Madison Guaranty Saving and Loan Association, the White Water Development Corporation, and other matters.[65]

- Deborah Gorham, Assistant to the Associate Counsel to the President, White House Office, appeared before the Senate Special Committee to Investigate the Whitewater Development Corporation and Related Matters on August 1, 1995, concerning whether White House staff had engaged in improper contacts regarding the Madison Guaranty Saving and Loan Association, the White Water Development Corporation, and other matters.[66]
- Carolyn C. Huber, Special Assistant to the President and Director of Personal Correspondence, White House Office, appeared before the Senate Special Committee to Investigate the Whitewater Development Corporation and Related Matters on August 3, 1995, and January 18, 1996, concerning whether White House staff had engaged in improper contacts regarding the Madison Guaranty Saving and Loan Association, the White Water Development Corporation, and other matters.[67]
- Harold Ickes, Deputy Chief of Staff, White House Office, appeared before the Senate Special Committee to Investigate the Whitewater Development Corporation and Related Matters on February 23, 1996, concerning whether White House staff had engaged in improper contacts regarding the Madison Guaranty Saving and Loan Association, the White Water Development Corporation, and other matters.[68]
- Evelyn Lieberman, Deputy Press Secretary for Operations, White House Office, appeared before the Senate Special Committee to Investigate the Whitewater Development Corporation and Related Matters on July 26, 1995, concerning whether White House staff had engaged in improper contacts regarding the Madison Guaranty Saving and Loan Association, the White Water Development Corporation, and other matters.[69]
- Bruce R. Lindsey, Assistant to the President and Deputy Counsel to the President, White House Office, appeared before the Senate Special Committee to Investigate the Whitewater Development Corporation and Related Matters on August 8 and November 28, 1995, and January 16, 1996, concerning whether White House staff had engaged in improper contacts regarding the Madison Guaranty Saving and Loan Association, the White Water Development Corporation, and other matters.[70]
- Capricia P. Marshall, Special Assistant to the First Lady, White House Office, appeared before the Senate Special Committee to Investigate

the Whitewater Development Corporation and Related Matters on February 9, 1996, concerning whether White House staff had engaged in improper contacts regarding the Madison Guaranty Saving and Loan Association, the White Water Development Corporation, and other matters.[71]

- Thomas F. McLarty III, Counsel to the President, White House Office, appeared before the Senate Special Committee to Investigate the Whitewater Development Corporation and Related Matters on August 7, 1995, concerning whether White House staff had engaged in improper contacts regarding the Madison Guaranty Saving and Loan Association, the White Water Development Corporation, and other matters.[72]
- Bobby J. Nash, Assistant to the President and Director of Presidential Personnel, White House Office, appeared before the Senate Special Committee to Investigate the Whitewater Development Corporation and Related Matters on January 31 and April 30, 1996, concerning whether White House staff had engaged in improper contacts regarding the Madison Guaranty Saving and Loan Association, the White Water Development Corporation, and other matters.[73]
- Stephen R. Neuwirth, Associate Counsel to the President, White House Office, appeared before the Senate Special Committee to Investigate the Whitewater Development Corporation and Related Matters on August 3, 1995, concerning whether White House staff had engaged in improper contacts regarding the Madison Guaranty Saving and Loan Association, the White Water Development Corporation, and other matters.[74]
- John M. Quinn, Assistant to the President and Chief of Staff to the Vice President, White House Office, appeared before the Senate Special Committee to Investigate the Whitewater Development Corporation and Related Matters on August 7, 1995, concerning whether White House staff had engaged in improper contacts regarding the Madison Guaranty Saving and Loan Association, the White Water Development Corporation, and other matters.[75]
- Jane C. Sherburne, Special Counsel to the President, White House Office, appeared before the Senate Special Committee to Investigate the Whitewater Development Corporation and Related Matters on November 9, 1995, and February 9, 1996, concerning whether White House staff had engaged in improper contacts regarding the Madison

Guaranty Saving and Loan Association, the White Water Development Corporation, and other matters.[76]

- Patti Solis, Special Assistant to the President and Director of Scheduling for the First Lady, appeared before the Senate Special Committee to Investigate the Whitewater Development Corporation and Related Matters on May 14, 1996, concerning whether White House staff had engaged in improper contacts regarding the Madison Guaranty Saving and Loan Association, the White Water Development Corporation, and other matters.[77]
- Patsy L. Thomasson, Deputy Assistant to the President and Assistant Director for Presidential Personnel, White House Office, appeared before the Senate Special Committee to Investigate the Whitewater Development Corporation and Related Matters on July 25, 1995, and May 9, 1996, concerning whether White House staff had engaged in improper contacts regarding the Madison Guaranty Saving and Loan Association, the White Water Development Corporation, and other matters.[78]
- Margaret A. Williams, Assistant to the President and Chief of Staff to the First Lady, White House Office, appeared before the Senate Special Committee to Investigate the Whitewater Development Corporation and Related Matters on July 26, November 2, and December 11, 1995, concerning whether White House staff had engaged in improper contacts regarding the Madison Guaranty Saving and Loan Association, the White Water Development Corporation, and other matters.[79]
- Charles Easley, Director of the Office of White House Security, White House Office, appeared before the Senate Committee on the Judiciary on June 28, 1996, concerning the dissemination of Federal Bureau of Investigation background investigation reports and other information to the White House.[80]
- Lanny Breuer, Special Counsel to the President, White House Office, appeared before the House Committee on Government Reform and Oversight on November 7, 1997, concerning White House compliance with committee subpoenas issued in the course of an investigation into alleged fund-raising abuses and the funneling of foreign money into political campaigns.[81]
- Cheryl Mills, Deputy Assistant to the President and Deputy Counsel to the President, White House Office, appeared before the House Committee on Government Reform and Oversight on November 6

and 7, 1997, concerning White House compliance with committee subpoenas issued in the course of an investigation into alleged fund-raising abuses and the funneling of foreign money into political campaigns.[82]

- Dimitri Nionakis, Associate Counsel to the President, White House Office, appeared before the House Committee on Government Reform and Oversight on November 7, 1997, concerning White House compliance with committee subpoenas issued in the course of an investigation into alleged fund-raising abuses and the funneling of foreign money into political campaigns.[83]
- Charles F. C. Ruff, Counsel to the President, White House Office, appeared before the House Committee on Government Reform and Oversight on November 6 and 7, 1997, concerning White House compliance with committee subpoenas issued in the course of an investigation into alleged fund-raising abuses and the funneling of foreign money into political campaigns.[84]
- Nancy Heinreich, Deputy Assistant to the President for Appointments and Scheduling, White House Office, appeared before the House Committee on Government Reform and Oversight on November 13, 1997, concerning the White House access and political campaign donations of Johnny Chung.[85]
- Mark Lindsay, Assistant to the President and Director of White House Management and Administration, White House Office, appeared before the House Committee on Government Reform on March 23, 2000, concerning White House mismanagement of its e-mail system and e-mails subpoenaed by the committee.[86]
- Dimitri Nionakis, Associate Counsel to the President, appeared before the House Committee on Government Reform on May 24, 2000, concerning White House mismanagement of its e-mail system and e-mails subpoenaed by the committee.[87]
- Beth Nolan, Counsel to the President, White House Office, appeared before the House Committee on Government Reform on March 30 and May 4, 2000, concerning White House mismanagement of its e-mail system and e-mails subpoenaed by the committee.[88]
- Thomas J. Ridge, Assistant to the President for Homeland Security, White House Office, appeared before the Senate Committee on Governmental Affairs on June 20, 2002, concerning the proposed Department of Homeland Security.[89]

- Thomas J. Ridge, Assistant to the President for Homeland Security, White House Office, appeared before the House Committee on Government Reform on June 20, 2002, concerning the proposed Department of Homeland Security.[90]
- Thomas J. Ridge, Assistant to the President for Homeland Security, White House Office, appeared before the House Committee on Energy and Commerce on June 26, 2002, concerning the proposed Department of Homeland Security.[91]
- Thomas J. Ridge, Assistant to the President for Homeland Security, White House Office, appeared before the Senate Committee on the Judiciary on June 26, 2002, concerning the proposed Department of Homeland Security.[92]
- Thomas J. Ridge, Assistant to the President for Homeland Security, White House Office, appeared before the House Committee on the Judiciary on June 26, 2002, concerning the proposed Department of Homeland Security.[93]
- Thomas J. Ridge, Assistant to the President for Homeland Security, White House Office, appeared before the Senate Committee on Environment and Public Works on July 10, 2002, concerning the proposed Department of Homeland Security.[94]
- Thomas J. Ridge, Assistant to the President for Homeland Security, White House Office, appeared before the House Select Committee on Homeland Security on July 15, 2002, concerning the proposed Department of Homeland Security.[95]
- Thomas J. Ridge, Assistant to the President for Homeland Security, White House Office, appeared before the Senate Committee on Health, Education, Labor, and Pensions on July 16, 2002, concerning the proposed Department of Homeland Security.[96]
- Thomas J. Ridge, Assistant to the President for Homeland Security, White House Office, appeared before the Senate Committee on Agriculture, Nutrition, and Forestry on July 17, 2002, concerning the proposed Department of Homeland Security.[97]
- J. Scott Jennings, Special Assistant to the President and Deputy White House Political Director, appeared before the Senate Committee on the Judiciary on August 2, 2007, concerning the dismissal of United States Attorneys.[98]

In a somewhat different case, Condoleezza Rice, Assistant to the President for National Security Affairs, after initially declining to testify, appeared before the National Commission on Terrorist Attacks Upon the United States on April 8, 2004, concerning the anti-terrorism efforts of the Bush Administration prior to the September 11, 2001, attacks upon the World Trade Center and the Pentagon.[99] Some viewed the commission as an independent entity because its membership was appointed by the President and the party leaders of Congress, while others noted that the panel's authorizing statute established it in the legislative branch.[100] On June 26, 2008, David S. Addington, Chief of Staff for Vice President Richard Cheney, testified before a subcommittee of the House Committee on the Judiciary concerning legal justification for harsh interrogation methods.[101]

Presidential Adviser Testimony Refused

Beginning with the years immediately after the conclusion of World War II, examples are provided below of instances when invited congressional committee or subcommittee testimony by a presidential adviser was refused. All examples are based upon the public record.

- John R. Steelman, Assistant to the President, White House Office, declined in March 1948 to appear before a special subcommittee of the House Committee on Education and Labor.[102]
- Herbert G. Klein, Director of White House Communications, White House Office, declined on September 21, 1971, to appear before the Senate Judiciary Subcommittee on Constitutional Rights.[103]
- Frederick V. Malek, Special Assistant to the President, White House Office, and Charles W. Colson, Special Counsel to the President, White House Office, declined in December 1971 to appear before the Senate Judiciary Subcommittee on Constitutional Rights.[104]
- Henry A. Kissinger, Assistant to the President for National Security Affairs, White House Office, declined on February 28, 1972, to appear before the Senate Committee on Foreign Relations.[105]
- David Young, Special Assistant to the National Security Council, declined on April 29, 1972, to appear before the House Government Operations Subcommittee on Foreign Operations and Government Information.[106]
- Thomas J. Ridge, Assistant to the President for Homeland Security, White House Office, declined March 15 and April 4, 2002, requests to appear before the Senate Committee on Appropriations.[107]

- Thomas J. Ridge, Assistant to the President for Homeland Security, White House Office, after declining to appear before the House Appropriations Subcommittee on Treasury, Postal Service, and General Government in late March, agreed to an informal, closed, April 10, 2002, meeting of subcommittee members.[108]
- Douglas Badger, Special Assistant to the President for Economic Policy, Office of Policy Development, declined on March 31, 2004, to appear before the House Committee on Ways and Means.[109]

Why Presidential Advisers Do Not Regularly Testify before Committees

"Although White House aides do not testify before congressional committees on a regular basis," it has been observed, "under certain conditions they do. First, intense and escalating political embarrassment may convince the White House that it is in the interest of the President to have these aides testify and ventilate the issue fully. Second, initial White House resistance may give way in the face of concerted congressional and public pressure."[110]

Given the comity between the executive and legislative branches, Congress often elects not to request the appearance of presidential aides.[111] When Congress has requested the appearance of such aides, Presidents and their aides have at times resisted, asserting the separation of powers doctrine and/or executive privilege.[112] These two grounds for declining to comply with congressional requests for the appearance of presidential aides overlap, and it is sometimes difficult to determine which argument is being raised.[113]

President Richard M. Nixon contended: "Under the doctrine of separation of powers, the manner in which the President personally exercises his assigned executive powers is not subject to questioning by another branch of Government. If the President is not subject to such questioning, it is equally appropriate that members of his staff not be so questioned, for their roles are in effect an extension of the Presidency."[114]

The separation of powers doctrine was also cited in guidelines for White House staff issued during the Carter Administration as the basis for the "immunity" of the staff from appearing before committees.[115] The guidelines "articulated the traditional arguments against compulsory testimony to Congress by White House advisers (i.e., need for 'frank and candid discussions,' personal advisers are agents of the President)."[116]

Executive privilege was invoked during the Nixon Administration when congressional committees sought the testimony of a White House aide at a Senate confirmation hearing[117] and the testimony of the White House Counsel at Senate committee hearings on the Watergate incident and related matters.[118]

Congress's Right to Executive Branch Information

Congress has a constitutionally rooted right of access to the information it needs to perform its Article I legislative and oversight functions.[119] Generally, a congressional committee with jurisdiction over the subject matter, which is conducting an authorized investigation for legislative or oversight purposes, has a right to information held by the executive branch in the absence of either a valid claim of constitutional privilege by the executive or a statutory provision whereby Congress has limited its constitutional right to information.[120]

Efforts by congressional committees to obtain information from the executive branch are sometimes met with assertions of executive privilege.[121] No decision of the Supreme Court resolves the question of whether there are any circumstances in which the executive branch can refuse to provide information sought by Congress on the basis of executive privilege, but the case law offers some guidance for committees when the privilege is asserted. In upholding a judicial subpoena in *United States v. Nixon*,[122] the Supreme Court found a constitutional basis for the doctrine of executive privilege,[123] rejected the President's contention that the privilege was absolute,[124] and balanced the President's need for confidentiality and the judiciary's need for the materials in a criminal proceeding.[125]

A distinction has been recognized by the courts between two aspects of executive privilege — the presidential communications privilege and the deliberative process privilege.[126] The former has a constitutional basis in the separation of powers doctrine and is rooted in concern for presidential decision making,[127] whereas the latter "is primarily a common law privilege" applicable "to decisionmaking of executive officials generally."[128] The former applies to entire documents (including factual material) and "covers final and postdecisional materials as well as predeliberative ones."[129] The latter covers predecisional and deliberative materials, not "purely factual [material], unless the material is so inextricably intertwined with the deliberative sections of documents that its disclosure would inevitably reveal the government's deliberations."[130] Both privileges are qualified.[131] When either privilege is asserted, the court will balance the public interests involved and assess the need of the party seeking the privileged information.[132]

The range of executive branch officials who may appropriately assert executive privilege before congressional committees, and the circumstances under which they may do so, remains unresolved by the courts[133] and is a matter that may be determined by case-by-case accommodation between the political branches.[134] Some guidance in this regard was offered byChief Justice William Rehnquist, when he was Assistant Attorney General in the Nixon Administration. Rehnquist distinguished between "those few executive branch witnesses whose sole responsibility is that of advising the President," who "should not be required to appear [before Congress] at all, since all of their official responsibilities would be subject to a claim of privilege," and "the executive branch witness ... whose responsibilities include the administration of departments or agencies established by Congress, and from whom Congress may quite properly require extensive testimony," subject to "appropriate" claims of privilege.[135]

Will a congressional request for the testimony of one who advises the President be honored? It is the view of the executive[136] that (1) the few individuals whose sole duty is to advise the President should never be required to testify because all of their duties are protected by executive privilege and (2) an official who has operational functions in a department or agency established by law may be required to testify, although at times such an official may invoke executive privilege. It is the view of the judiciary that the presidential communications privilege should be restricted to White House advisers when "preparing advice for the President.... "[137]

PROCEDURE FOR OBTAINING EXECUTIVE BRANCH TESTIMONY

A congressional committee may request (informally or by a letter from the committee chair, perhaps cosigned by the ranking Member) or demand (pursuant to subpoena[138]) the testimony of a presidential adviser. However, Congress may encounter legal and political problems in attempting to enforce a subpoena to a presidential adviser.

Conflicts concerning congressional requests or demands for executive branch testimony or documents often involve extensive negotiations, and may be resolved by some form of compromise as to, inter alia, the scope of the testimony or information to be provided to Congress.[139] If the executive branch fails to comply with a committee subpoena, and if negotiations do not resolve the matter, the committee may employ Congress's inherent contempt authority (involving a trial at the bar of the Senate or House) or statutory criminal contempt authority in an effort to obtain the needed information.[140] Both of these procedures are somewhat cumbersome, and their use may not result in the production of the information that is sought.[141]

When faced with a refusal by the executive branch to comply with a demand for information, Congress has several alternatives to inherent and statutory contempt, although these alternatives are not without their own limitations.[142] One approach is to seek declaratory or other relief in the courts. Previous attempts to seek judicial resolution of interbranch conflicts over information access issues have encountered procedural obstacles and have demonstrated the reluctance of the courts to resolve sensitive separation of powers issues.[143] Other approaches may include, inter alia, appropriations riders, impeachment, and a delay in the confirmation of presidential appointees.[144]

In addition to the options generally available in the event of a refusal by the executive to provide information sought by Congress, when a presidential adviser who is not serving in a department or agency established by law declines to testify before a committee, Congress might wish to enact legislation establishing the entity and making the head of the entity subject to Senate confirmation.[145]

CONCLUSION

(1) Legal and policy factors may explain why presidential advisers do not regularly testify before committees. (2) Generally, a congressional committee with jurisdiction over the subject matter, which is conducting an authorized investigation for legislative or oversight purposes, has a right to information held by the executive branch in the absence of either a valid claim of constitutional privilege by the executive or a statutory provision whereby Congress has limited its constitutional right to information. (3) A committee may request or demand the testimony of a presidential adviser. Legal mechanisms available for enforcing congressional subpoenas to the executive

branch may fail to provide the committee with the desired information. (4) Negotiations may result in the production of at least some of the information sought.

End Notes

[1] Andrew A. Lipscomb and Albert Ellery Bergh, eds., *The Writings of Thomas Jefferson,* vol. 1 (Washington: Thomas Jefferson Memorial Association, 1903), pp. 303-304.

[2] Arthur M. Schlesinger, Jr., *The Age of Jackson* (Boston, MA: Little, Brown, 1945), p. 67.

[3] Louis W. Koenig, *The Invisible Presidency* (New York: Rinehart, 1960), p. 40.

[4] 4 Stat. 633.

[5] 11 Stat. 228.

[6] 45 Stat. 1230.

[7] See Rexford G. *Tugwell, The Brains Trust* (New York: Viking, 1968).

[8] Samuel I. Rosenman, ed., *The Public Papers and Addresses of Franklin D. Roosevelt, Volume 5: The People Approve, 1936* (New York: Random House, 1938), p. 144.

[9] U.S. President's Committee on Administrative Management, *Report of the President's Committee* (Washington: GPO, 1937), p. 5.

[10] 53 Stat. 561.

[11] Richard Polenberg, *Reorganizing Roosevelt's Government* (Cambridge, MA: Harvard University Press, 1966), pp. 184-187.

[12] 53 Stat. 1423.

[13] 53 Stat. 1431 at 1435.

[14] 53 Stat. 813.

[15] 3 C.F.R., 1938-1943 Comp., pp. 576-579.

[16] Louis Brownlow, *A Passion for Anonymity: The Autobiography of Louis Brownlow, Second Half* (Chicago, IL: University of Chicago Press, 1958), p. 416.

[17] 3 C.F.R., 1938-1943 Comp., pp. 1320-1321.

[18] *Weekly Compilation of Presidential Documents*, vol. 9, January 8, 1973, p. 7.

[19] 58 Stat. 387.

[20] 96 Stat. 877 at 925, 1076.

[21] Established by E.O. 9024 of January 16, 1942, the War Production Board was technically located within the Office for Emergency Management, an agency within the Executive Office of the President, but it operated independently as an arm of the President. The chairman of the board was presidentially appointed without Senate confirmation; eight other specified government officials were members of the board. The board was terminated by E.O. 9638 of October 4, 1945.

[22] Donald M. Nelson, *Arsenal of Democracy: The Story of American War Production* (New York: Harcourt, Brace, 1946), pp. 128, 332; Donald H. Riddle, *The Truman Committee: A Study in Congressional Responsibility* (New Brunswick, NJ: Rutgers University Press, 1964), pp. 36, 70, 83-84.

[23] Herman Miles Somers, *Presidential Agency: The Office of War Mobilization and Reconversion* (Cambridge, MA: Harvard University Press, 1950), p. 74.

[24] U.S. Congress, Senate Committee on Agriculture and Forestry, *Administration of the Rural Electrification Act,* hearings, 78th Cong., 2nd sess. (Washington: GPO, 1944), pp. 611ff, 695ff, 721ff.

[25] U.S. Congress, Senate Committee on Appropriations, *Speculation in Commodity Markets*, hearings, 80th Cong., 2nd sess. (Washington: GPO, 1948), pp. 49ff.

[26] U.S. Congress, Senate Committee on Expenditures in the Executive Departments, *Influence in Government Procurement,* hearings, 81st Cong., 1st sess. (Washington: GPO, 1949), pp. 495ff, 563ff.

[27] U.S. Congress, Senate Committee on Banking and Currency, *Study of Reconstruction Finance Corporation,* hearings, 82nd Cong., 1st sess. (Washington: GPO, 1951), pp. 1709ff, 1795ff.

[28] U.S. Congress, House Committee on Interstate and Foreign Commerce, *Investigation of Regulatory Commissions and Agencies,* hearings, 85th Cong., 2nd sess. (Washington: GPO, 1958), p. 3712 ff.

[29] U.S. Congress, Senate Committee on Interior and Insular Affairs, *The President's Energy Message,* hearings, 92nd Cong., 1st sess. (Washington: GPO, 1971), p. 12ff; U.S. Congress, House Committee on Science and Astronautics, *U.S.-U.S.S.R. Cooperative Agreements,* hearings, 92nd Cong., 2nd sess (Washington: GPO, 1972), p. 60ff.

[30] U.S. Congress, House Select Committee on Small Business, *Advertising and Small Business,* hearings, 92nd Cong., 1st sess. (Washington: GPO, 1971), p. 567ff.

[31] U.S. Congress, House Committee on Interstate and Foreign Commerce, *Special Action Office for Drug Abuse Prevention*, hearings, 92nd Cong., 1st sess. (Washington: GPO, 1971), pp. 171ff, 1037ff, 1443, 1578ff.

[32] U.S. Congress, Senate Committee on the Judiciary, *Nominations of Richard G. Kleindienst and L. Patrick Gray III,* hearings, 92nd Cong., 2nd sess (Washington: GPO, 1972), p. 1585ff.

[33] U.S. Congress, Senate Select Committee on *Presidential Campaign Activities, Presidential Campaign Activities of 1972*, hearings, 93rd Cong., 1st sess. (Washington: GPO, 1973), p. 75ff.

[34] Ibid., p. 3899ff.

[35] U.S. Congress, Senate Committee on Appropriations, *Treasury, Postal Service, and General Government Appropriations: Fiscal Year 1978,* hearings, 95th Cong., 1st sess. (Washington: GPO, 1977), p. 1021ff; U.S. Congress, House Committee on Appropriations, *Treasury, Postal Service, and General Government Appropriations for Fiscal Year 1978,* hearings, 95th Cong., 1st sess. (Washington: GPO, 1977), p. 77ff.

[36] U.S. Congress, Senate Select Committee on *Presidential Campaign Activities, Presidential Campaign Activities of 1972*, hearings, 93rd Cong., 2nd sess. (Washington: GPO, 1974), p. 10193ff.

[37] Ibid., pp. 10539ff, 10877ff.

[38] Ibid., pp. 10849ff, 10998ff.

[39] Ibid., p. 11053ff.

[40] U.S. Congress, Senate Committee on the Judiciary, *Inquiry into the Matter of Billy Carter and Libya*, hearings, 96th Cong., 2nd sess. (Washington: GPO, 1981), p. 1195ff.

[41] Ibid., p. 1339ff.

[42] *Congressional Record,* Daily Digest, vol. 140, May 3, 1994, p. D245.

[43] U.S. Congress, Senate Committee on Governmental Affairs, *Investigation of Illegal or Improper Activities in Connection with the 1996 Federal Election Campaign,* hearings, 105th Cong., 1st sess. (Washington: GPO, 1998), p. 204ff.

[44] U.S. Congress, House Committee on Banking, Finance, and Urban Affairs, *White House Contacts with Treasury/RTC Officials About "Whitewater"-Related Matters,* part 1, hearing, 103rd Cong., 2nd sess. (Washington: GPO, 1994), p. 12ff.

[45] Ibid., part 2, p. 104ff.

[46] Ibid., p. 108ff.

[47] Ibid., p. 103ff.

[48] Ibid., p. 105ff.

[49] Ibid., p. 100ff.

[50] Ibid., p. 112ff.

[51] Ibid., p. 100ff.

[52] Ibid., p. 111ff.

[53] Ibid., p. 109ff.

54 U.S. Congress, Senate Committee on Banking, Housing, and Urban Affairs, *Hearings Relating to Madison Guaranty S&L and the Whitewater Development Corporation — Washington DC Phase*, vol. 4, hearings, 103rd Cong., 2nd sess. (Washington: GPO, 1995), p. 734ff.
55 Ibid., p. 87ff.
56 Ibid., p. 353ff.
57 Ibid., p. 86ff.
58 Ibid., p. 357ff.
59 Ibid., p. 270ff.
60 Ibid., p. 89ff.
61 Ibid., p. 360ff.
62 Ibid., p. 88ff.
63 Ibid., p. 360ff.
64 Ibid., p. 272ff.
65 *Congressional Record,* vol. 141, July 25, 1995, p. D493; although the transcripts of the hearings held by the Senate Special Committee have not been published, a committee list of those who testified before the panel is in the possession of the author.
66 Ibid., August 1, 1995, p. D519.
67 Ibid., August 3, 1995, p. D532; Ibid., vol. 142, January 18, 1996, p. D10.
68 Ibid., vol. 142, February 23, 1996, p. D39.
69 Ibid., vol. 141, July 26, 1995, p. D499.
70 Ibid., August 8, 1995, p. D547; Ibid., November 28, 1995, p. D747; Ibid., vol. 142, January 16, 1996, p. D10.
71 Ibid., vol. 142, February 9, 196, p. D35.
72 Ibid., vol. 141, August 7, 1995, p. D544.
73 Ibid., vol. 142, January 31, 1996, p. D22; Ibid., April 30, 1996, p. D195.
74 Ibid., vol. 141, August 3, 1995, p. D532.
75 Ibid., August 7, 1995, p. D544.
76 Ibid., November 9, 1995, p. D721; Ibid., vol. 142, February 9, 1996, p. D35.
77 Ibid., vol. 142, May 14, 1996, p. D236.
78 Ibid., vol. 141, July 25, 1995, p. D493; Ibid., vol. 142, May 9, 1996, p. D227.
79 Ibid., vol. 141, July 26, 1995, p. D499; Ibid., November 2, 1995, p. D707; Ibid., December 11, 1995, p. D774.
80 Ibid., vol. 142, June 28, 1996, p. D362.
81 U.S. Congress, House Committee on Government Reform and Oversight, *White House Compliance with Committee Subpoenas*, hearings, 105th Cong., 1st sess. (Washington: GPO, 1998), p. 219ff.
82 Ibid., pp. 51ff, 157ff.
83 Ibid., p. 218ff.
84 Ibid., pp. 44ff, 152f.
85 U.S. Congress, House Committee on Government Reform and Oversight, *Johnny Chung: His Unusual Access to the White House, His Political Donations, and Related Matters*, hearings, 105th Cong., 1st sess. (Washington: GPO, 1998), p. 705ff.
86 U.S. Congress, House Committee on Government Reform, *Missing White House E-mails: Mismanagement of Subpoenaed Records,* hearings, 106th Cong., 2nd sess. (Washington: GPO, 2001), p. 137ff.
87 Ibid., p. 769ff.
88 Ibid., pp. 262ff, 769ff.
89 U.S. Congress, Senate Committee on Governmental Affairs, *President Bush's Proposal to Create a Department of Homeland Security*, hearing, 107th Cong., 2nd sess. (Washington: GPO, 2002), p. 25ff.
90 U.S. Congress, House Committee on Government Reform, *The Department of Homeland Security: An Overview of the President's Proposal*, hearing, 107th Cong., 2nd sess. (Washington: GPO, 2002), p. 85ff.

[91] U.S. Congress, House Committee on Energy and Commerce, *Creating the Department of Homeland Security: Consideration of the Administration's Proposal,* hearings, 107th Cong., 2nd sess. (Washington: GPO, 2002), p. 14ff.

[92] *Congressional Record*, v. 148, June 26, 2002, p. D687.

[93] U.S. Congress, House Committee on the Judiciary, *Homeland Security Act of 2002,* hearing, 107th Cong. 2nd sess. (Washington: GPO, 2002), p. 5ff.

[94] *Congressional Record,* v. 148, July 10, 2002, p. D730.

[95] U.S. Congress, House Select Committee on Homeland Security, *H.R. 5005, the Homeland Security Act of 2002, Days 1 and 2*, hearings, 107th Cong., 2nd sess. (Washington: GPO, 2002), p. 7ff.

[96] U.S. Congress, Senate Committee on Health, Education, Labor, and Pensions, *Homeland Security*, hearing, 107th Cong., 2nd sess. (Washington: GPO, 2002), p. 8ff.

[97] *Congressional Record*, v. 148, July 17, 2002, p. D768.

[98] Paul Kane, "Bush Aide Addresses Missing RNC E-Mails," *Washington Post,* August 3, 2007, p. A2; Neil A. Lewis, "White House Aide Won't Answer Questions of a Senate Panel," *New York Times,* August 3, 2007, p. A13.

[99] James G. Lakely, "Al Qaeda a Target Early, Rice Says," *Washington Times*, April 9, 2004, pp. A1, A13; Dan Eggen and Walter Pincus, "Rice Defends Pre-9/11 Anti-Terrorism Efforts: U.S. 'Was Not on War Footing,' She Says," *Washington Post,* April 9, 2004, pp. A1, A10.

[100] See 116 Stat. 2408.

[101] Dan Eggen, "Bush Policy Authors Defend Their Actions," *Washington Post,* June 27, 2008, p. A2; Scott Shane, "Two Testify on Memo Spelling Out Interrogation," *New York Times*, June 27, 2008, p. A15.

[102] U.S. Congress, House Committee on Education and Labor, *Investigation of the GSA Strike,* hearings, 80th Cong., 2nd sess. (Washington: GPO, 1948), pp. 347-353.

[103] U.S. Congress, Senate Committee on the Judiciary, Freedom of the Press, hearings, 92nd Cong., 1st and 2nd sess. (Washington: GPO, 1972), p. 1299.

[104] Ibid., p. 425.

[105] *Congressional Record,* vol. 118, March 28, 1972, p. 10471; Kissinger "occasionally talked on the phone, or privately met, with top legislative leaders, briefed them at pro forma consultations before major military actions or on the occasion of big diplomatic agreements, and once in a while informally briefed larger congressional groups. Kissinger would go to the Hill, incognito as it were, a couple of times a year and he might entertain a congressional group in the OEOB [Old Executive Office Building] maybe once a year. In some of the sessions that did occur the Congress was misinformed on key issues ... in the cases of the Vietnam peace agreement and the first SALT agreements with the Soviets." John Prados, Keepers of the Keys: *A History of the National Security Council from Truman to Bush* (New York: William Morrow, 1991), p. 309.

[106] U.S. Congress, House Committee on Government Operations, *U.S. Government Information Policies and Practices — Security Classification Problems Involving (b)(1) of the Freedom of Information Act*, hearings, 92nd Cong., 2nd sess. (Washington: GPO, 1972), p. 2453.

[107] Associated Press, "Ridge Won't Tell Senate His Views on the War," *Washington Times,* March 5, 2002, p. A3; Alison Mitchell, "Congressional Hearings: Letter to Ridge Is Latest Jab in Fight Over Balance of Powers," *New York Times,* March 5, 2002, p. A8; Mark Preston, "Byrd Holds Firm," *Roll Call*, April 18, 2002, pp. 1, 26, 28.

[108] George Archibald, "Panel Ties Funding to Ridge Testimony," *Washington Times,* March 22, 2002, pp. A1, A14; George Archibald, "White House Mollifies House Panel," *Washington Times,* March 23, 2002, A1, A4; Elizabeth Becker, "Domestic Security: Ridge Briefs House Panel, but Discord Is Not Resolved," *New York Times*, April 11, 2002, p. A17.

[109] Amy Goldstein, "Democrats Ask Bush Aides to Explain Role on Medicare Cost," *Washington Post,* March 20, 2004, p. A5; "Ways and Means Republicans Allow Scully, White House to Avoid Answering Questions on Medicare Estimate Coverup," News Release from Rep. Charles B. Rangel, Committee on Ways and Means, April 1, 2004.

[110] Louis Fisher, "White House Aides Testifying before Congress," *Presidential Studies Quarterly*, vol. 27, Winter 1997, p. 139.
[111] Ibid., p. 151.
[112] Ibid., pp. 140-141.
[113] In two instances during the Carter Administration, when presidential advisers declined to appear before committees, objections were raised which are difficult to categorize. *See* Mark J. Rozell, "Executive Privilege and the Modern Presidents: In Nixon's Shadow," *Minnesota Law Review*, vol. 83, May 1999, pp. 1069, 1090-1091, 1092.
The Bush Administration resisted congressional attempts to secure the testimony of Tom Ridge, Assistant to the President for Homeland Security. The Administration invoked the separation of powers doctrine ("Ridge Will Not Give Congress His Testimony," *USA Today*, March 25, 2002, p. 7A), and stated that Ridge would not appear because he was a presidential adviser, not a Cabinet officer, and because he was not confirmed by the Senate. The Bush Administration also contended that the President, rather than Congress, oversees a presidential adviser who is not confirmed by the Senate. "A Nation Challenged: Congressional Hearings," *New York Times*, March 5, 2002, p. 8; "Congress, White House Fight Over Ridge Status," *Washington Post*, March 21, 2002, p. A33. However, some Members argued that Ridge's position was new and unique, and that he had influence over multiple departments whose budgets were subject to Congress's power of the purse. "Backlash Grows Against White House Secrecy," *Christian Science Monitor,* March 25, 2002, p. 3.
[114] Fisher, "White House Aides Testifying before Congress," p. 140 (quoting *Public Papers of the President, 1973* (Washington: GPO, 1975), at p. 160). The separation of powers doctrine was also cited by the Carter Administration as the rationale for White House advisers not appearing before Congress. Rozell, "Executive Privilege and the Modern Presidents: In Nixon's Shadow," pp. 1091-1092.
[115] Rozell, "Executive Privilege and the Modern Presidents: In Nixon's Shadow," p. 1091 and note 116 (citing to memorandum of February 8, 1979, from Robert Lipshutz to White House staff).
[116] Ibid., p.1091 and note 15 (citing to Lipshutz memorandum).
[117] Fisher, "White House Aides Testifying before Congress," p. 140.
[118] Ibid., pp. 140-141.
[119] *See McGrain* v. *Daugherty,* 273 U.S. 135, 177, 181-182 (1927). In a frequently quoted passage, the Court explained, at p. 174:
A legislative body cannot legislate wisely or effectively in the absence of information respecting the conditions which the legislation is intended to affect or change; and where the legislative body does not itself possess the requisite information — which not infrequently is true — recourse must be had to others who do possess it. Experience has taught that mere requests for such information often are unavailing, and also that information which is volunteered is not always accurate or complete; so some means of compulsion are essential to obtain what is needed. All this was true before and when the Constitution was framed and adopted. In that period the power of inquiry — with enforcing process — was regarded and employed as a necessary and appropriate attribute of the power to legislate — indeed, was treated as inhering in it. Thus there is ample warrant for thinking, as we do, that the constitutional provisions which commit the legislative function to the two houses are intended to include this attribute to the end that the function may be effectively exercised.
See also Watkins v. United States, 354 U.S. 178, 200 note 33 (1957). For a more detailed discussion of the constitutional and statutory authority for congressional access to information and for an examination of related issues, see CRS Report RL30240, *Congressional Oversight Manual.*
[120] *See Wilkinson* v. *United States*, 365 U.S. 399, 408-409 (1961); Congressional Oversight Manual, supra note 117.

[121] For a more detailed analysis of the doctrine of executive privilege in the context of congressional investigations, see CRS Report RL30319, *Presidential Claims of Executive Privilege: History, Law, Practice and Recent Developments*, by Morton Rosenberg. See also Louis Fisher, *The Politics of Executive Privilege* (Durham, NC: Carolina Academic Press, 2004).

[122] 418 U.S. 683 (1974). The subpoena, issued to the President at the request of the Watergate Special Prosecutor, demanded tape recordings of confidential conversations between the President and his advisors. Ibid., p. 703.

[123] The Court found the basis in "the supremacy of each branch within its own assigned area of constitutional duties" and in the separation of powers. Ibid., pp. 705, 706. See also ibid., pp. 708, 711. The Court also found the privilege to be rooted in the President's need for confidentiality. Ibid., p. 708.

[124] Ibid., p. 708. The Court considered presidential communications to be "presumptively privileged" (ibid., p. 705). Because the privilege is not absolute, judicial review is available. Ibid., 708.

[125] Ibid., p. 707. The Court resolved the "competing interests" so as to preserve "the essential functions of each branch." Ibid. Under the circumstances of the case, the judicial need for the tapes outweighed the President's "generalized interest in confidentiality...." Ibid., p. 713. The Court was careful to limit the scope of its decision (ibid., p. 712 n.19), noting that it was not addressing a case involving a congressional demand for information or a case involving the President's interest in preserving state secrets. The Court appeared to be willing to accord greater protection to "military, diplomatic, or sensitive national security secrets" (ibid., p. 706) than it was to a President's communications with his advisers.

United States v. *Nixon* did not involve a presidential claim of executive privilege in response to a congressional subpoena. In *Senate Select Committee on Presidential Campaign Activities* v. *Nixon*, 498 F.2d 725 (D.C. Cir. 1974), the court reviewed the President's assertion of executive privilege as grounds for not complying with a committee subpoena for tape recordings of conversations between the President and his staff. The court found that "the presumption that the public interest favors confidentiality [in presidential communications] can be defeated only by a strong showing of need by another institution of government.... " Ibid., p. 730. Under the unusual circumstances of that case, the court found that the legislative and oversight needs of the committee were insufficient to overcome the claim of privilege. Ibid., p. 732.

[126] *In re Sealed Case (Espy)*, 121 F.3d 729 (D.C. Cir. 1997). For an analysis of *Espy*, see Rozell, "Executive Privilege and the Modern Presidents: In Nixon's Shadow," pp. 11191120.

[127] *Espy*, 121 F.3d at 745, 752. Confidential advice is critical to presidential decision making. Ibid., p. 751. To limit the privilege to its purpose (protecting "the confidentiality of the President's decision making process"), *Espy* construed the privilege narrowly. Ibid., p. 752. Espy held that the presidential communications privilege "extends to communications authored by or solicited and received by presidential advisers" when "preparing advice for the President," "even when these communications are not made directly to the President." Ibid., pp. 751-752, 762. *Espy* restricted the privilege to White House advisers with "operational proximity" to the President (ibid., p. 752) and found that the privilege "should not extend to staff outside the White House in executive branch agencies." Ibid. The privilege does not apply to White House advisers when they "exercise substantial independent authority or perform other functions in addition to advising the President.... " Ibid.

At issue in *Espy* was a grand jury subpoena for documents pertaining to an investigation by the White House Counsel. The documents "were generated in the course of advising the President in the exercise of his appointment and removal power, a quintessential and nondelegable presidential power." Ibid.

The *Espy* court emphasized that its "opinion should not be read as in any way affecting the scope of the [presidential communications] privilege in the congressional-executive

context.... The President's ability to withhold information from Congress implicates different constitutional considerations than the President's ability to withhold evidence in judicial proceedings." Ibid., p. 753. Furthermore, the court in *Espy* noted that its "determination of how far down into the executive branch the presidential communications privilege goes" was limited to the circumstances of the case. Ibid.
Arguably, the privilege must be asserted by the President personally. Ibid, p. 745 note 16 (collecting cases).

[128] Ibid., p. 745.

[129] Ibid.

[130] Ibid., p. 737.

[131] Ibid., p. 746. The presidential communications privilege is more difficult to overcome, requiring the party seeking the information to "provide a focused demonstration of need...." Ibid. "The [deliberative process] privilege disappears altogether when there is any reason to believe government misconduct occurred.... A party seeking to overcome the presidential privilege seemingly must always provide a focused demonstration of need, even when there are allegations of misconduct by high-level officials." Ibid.

[132] Ibid.

[133] *Cf. In re Lindsey,* 158 F.3d 1263, 1277-1278 (D.C. Cir.) *(dictum), cert denied sub nom. Office of the President* v. *Office of Independent Counsel*, 525 U.S. 996 (1998).

[134] *See* Dawn Johnsen, "Executive Privilege Since *United States v. Nixon: Issues of Motivation and Accommodation," vol. 83, Minnesota Law Review,* May 1999, p. 1127ff.

[135] U.S. Congress, Senate Committee on the Judiciary, Subcommittee on Separation of Powers, *Executive Privilege: The Withholding of Information by the Executive,* hearings, 92nd Cong., 1st Sess. (Washington: GPO, 1971), p. 427 (hereafter, Rehnquist statement).

[136] *See* Rehnquist's statement (*supra* text accompanying note 133) and the discussion of the precedents and practice concerning congressional access to executive branch information, particularly the testimony of presidential advisers) (*supra* notes 110 to 116 and accompanying text).

[137] *See Espy*, 121 F.3d at 751-752.

[138] Standing committees of both the Senate (Rule XXVI(1)) and the House (Rule XI, cl. 2(m)) have subpoena power.

[139] A presidential adviser may provide information to a committee in a hearing (answering questions of members of a committee under applicable rules of the House or the committee), in an informal briefing (with only the chairman or with a few or all committee members), or in a deposition. *See*, e.g., Fisher, "White House Aides Testifying before Congress," p. 139. The appearance of a presidential adviser before a committee may be open to the public or it may be closed. His testimony at a hearing may be sworn or unsworn.
In response to congressional attempts to secure the testimony of Ridge (*see supra* note 113), Ridge offered to brief Members privately, but some Members objected. Subsequently, Ridge offered to brief Members of both the Senate and the House informally, but in public. Ridge argued that his proposal would satisfy congressional needs but "avoid the setting of a precedent that could undermine the constitutional separation of powers and the longstanding traditions and practices of both Congress and the executive branch." "A Nation Challenged: The Security Director," *New York Times,* March 26, 2002, p. 13. Ridge said that he would meet with Members in "briefings" but not in "hearings." Louis Fisher, *The Politics of Executive Privilege* (Durham, NC: Carolina Academic Press, 2004), p. 226.
Although the focus of this report is on issues raised by the testimony of presidential advisers before congressional committees, their testimony before other legislative branch entities raises similar issues. Condoleezza Rice, Assistant to the President for National Security Affairs, appeared twice before the National Commission on Terrorist Attacks Upon the United States. The commission, which reported to the Congress and the President, may be viewed as a legislative body because it was established in the legislative branch and because

nine of its 10 members were appointed by the congressional leadership. Act of November 27, 2002, P.L. 107-306, 116 Stat. 2408 (amended 2004), 6 U.S.C. § 101 note. Rice was interviewed privately by the commission on February 7, 2004. "Refusal to Testify Has Precedent," *Washington Post*, March 27, 2004, p. A10. Although the Bush Administration at first argued that her appearance in public might prevent the President from receiving the "best and most candid possible advice," she subsequently testified in public and under oath on April 8, 2004. "Talking About Secrets," *Legal Times,* April 19, 2004, p. 66.

[140] Both the inherent contempt power and the statutory procedure (2 U.S.C. 192, 194) are outlined in CRS Report RL30240, *Congressional Oversight Manual.* The statutory civil contempt procedure which may be used by Senate committees is not applicable in the case of an executive branch official. 28 U.S.C. 1365.

[141] See Randall K. Miller, "Congressional Inquests: Suffocating the Constitutional Prerogative of Executive Privilege," vol. 81, *Minnesota Law Review*, February 1997, pp. 631, 658.

[142] For a overview and evaluation of the alternatives, see J. Richard Broughton, "Paying Ambition's Debt: Can the Separation of Powers Tame the Impetuous Vortex of Congressional Investigations?," vol. 21, *Whittier Law Review,* 2000, pp. 797, 825-832. See also Roberto Iraola, "Congressional Oversight, Executive Privilege, and Requests for Information Relating to Federal Criminal Investigations and Prosecutions," vol. 87, Iowa Law Review, August 2002, p. 1559ff.

[143] *Senate Select Committee v. Nixon,* 498 F.2d 725 (D.C. Cir. 1974); United States v. AT&T, 551 F.2d 384 (D.C. Cir. 1976) and 567 F.2d 121 (D.C. Cir. 1977) (second opinion); *United States v. House of Representatives,* 556 F. Supp. 150 (D.D.C. 1983).

[144] See, e.g., Broughton, "Paying Ambition's Debt: Can the Separation of Powers Tame the Impetuous Vortex of *Congressional Investigations?," pp. 831-835; Louis Fisher, Constitutional Conflicts between Congress and the President*, 4th ed (Lawrence, KS: University Press of Kansas, 1997), pp. 183-184. In response to the resistance of the Bush Administration to congressional attempts to obtain the testimony of Ridge (*see supra* note 111), it was reported that the House Appropriations Committee considered a delay in acting on the appropriation for the Executive Office of the President. "Panel Ties Funding to Ridge Testimony," *Washington Times*, March 22, 2002, pp. A1, A14.

[145] As discussed above (*see supra* p. 27), an executive branch official who administers a department or agency established by law is generally expected to testify before committees, in contrast to an individual whose sole responsibility is to advise the President. Some presidential advisers are in units of the Executive Office of the President established by law, and are also subject to confirmation by the Senate. *See,* e.g., 15 U.S.C. 1023 (Council of Economic Advisors); 42 U.S.C. 4321, 4372 (Office of Environmental Quality); 42 U.S.C. 6611, 6612 (Office of Science and Technology Policy); 31 U.S.C. 501, 502 (Office of Management and Budget (OMB)).

To increase its oversight of OMB, Congress passed legislation subjecting the Director to Senate confirmation, notwithstanding the objections of the Nixon Administration. See Donald S. Onley, "Treading on Sacred Ground: Congress's Power to Subject White House Advisers to Senate Confirmation," vol. 37, *William & Mary Law Review,* Spring 1996, pp. 1183-1184. Congress' constitutional authority over offices and officeholders is limited by separation of powers considerations and by constitutional powers of the President. *See ibid.*, pp. 1187-1214. See also Aaron-Andrew Bruhl, "Using Statutes to Set Legislative Rules: Entrenchment, Separation of Powers, and the Rules of Proceedings Clause," vol. 19, *Journal of Law & Politics*, Fall 2003, pp. 345, 375 note 238. By subjecting a presidential adviser to confirmation by the Senate, Congress may obtain practical, although not necessarily legal leverage, in attempting to secure his testimony. *See generally* Louis Fisher, "Executive Privilege and the Bush Administration: Congressional Access to Information — -Using Legislative Will and Leverage," vol. 52, *Duke Law Journal,* November 2002, p. 323.

The Bush Administration resisted congressional attempts to have Tom Ridge, the Director of the Office of Homeland Security, testify. *See supra* note 113. The Office of Homeland Security was established within the Executive Office of the President pursuant to E.O. 13228, issued on October 8, 2001. *Federal Register,* vol. 66, October 10, 2001, pp. 51812-51817. Even before Congress requested Ridge's testimony, legislation had been introduced to create an office with homeland security functions. *See, e.g.*, S. 1449, 107th Cong. (to establish within the White House a National Office for Combating Terrorism, with a director subject to Senate confirmation); S. 1534, 107th Cong. (to establish a "Department of National Homeland Security," with the Secretary subject to Senate confirmation). Upon the introduction of S. 1534, Sen. Joseph Lieberman observed that the Secretary "will be accountable to the Congress and the American people." *Congressional Record,* daily edition, vol. 147. October 10, 2001, p. S10646. Ultimately, Congress established the Department of Homeland Security. P.L. 107-296, § 101, 116 Stat. 2135 (2002). Ridge's nomination as the first Secretary of the new department was approved subject to his "commitment to respond to requests to appear and testify before any duly constituted committee of the Senate." *Congressional Record,* daily edition, vol. 149, January 22, 2003, p. S1372.

Chapter Sources

The following chapters have been previously published:

Chapter 1 - This is an edited, reformatted and augmented version of a Congressional Research Service publication, Report Order Code RL30319, updated April 16, 2008.

Chapter 2 – This is an edited, reformatted and augmented version of a Congressional Research Service publication, Report Order Code RL31351, updated July 16, 2008.

INDEX

#

A

B

C

D

E

F

G

H

I

S

T

U